CONTEMPORARY RUSSIAN NOVELISTS

CONTEMPORARY RUSSIAN NOVELISTS

By

SERGE PERSKY

Translated by Frederick Eisemann

Essay Index Reprint Series

 BOOKS FOR LIBRARIES PRESS
FREEPORT, NEW YORK

First Published 1913
Reprinted 1968

891.709
P 43 c
6 5 5 6 3
April 1969

LIBRARY OF CONGRESS CATALOG CARD NUMBER:

68-26468

PRINTED IN THE UNITED STATES OF AMERICA

PREFACE

THE principal aim of this book is to give the reader a good general knowledge of Russian literature as it is to-day. The author, Serge Persky, has subordinated purely critical material, because he wants his readers to form their own judgments and criticize for themselves. The element of literary criticism is not, however, by any means entirely lacking.

In the original text, there is a thorough and exhaustive treatment of the " great prophet " of Russian literature — Tolstoy — but the translator has deemed it wise to omit this essay, because so much has recently been written about this great man.

As the title of the book is " Contemporary Russian Novelists," the essay on Anton Tchekoff, who is no longer living, does not rightly belong here, but Tchekoff is such an important figure in modern Russian literature and has attracted so little attention from English writers that it seems advisable to retain the essay that treats of his work.

Finally, let me express my sincerest thanks to Dr. G. H. Maynadier of Harvard for his kind advice; to Miss Edna Wetzler for her unfailing and valuable help, and to Miss Carrie Harper, who has gone over this work with painstaking care.

CONTENTS

CONTENTS

CONTEMPORARY RUSSIAN NOVELISTS

I

A BRIEF SURVEY OF RUSSIAN LITERATURE

In order to get a clear idea of modern Russian literature, a knowledge of its past is indispensable. This knowledge will help us in understanding that which distinguishes it from other European literatures, not only from the viewpoint of the art which it expresses, but also as the historical and sociological mirror of the nation's life in the course of centuries.

The dominant trait of this literature is found in its very origins. Unlike the literatures of other European countries, which followed, in a more or less regular way, the development of life and civilization during historic times, Russian literature passed through none of these stages. Instead of being a product of the past, it is a protestation against it; instead of retracing the old successive stages, it appears, in-

1

termittently, like a light suddenly struck in the
darkness. Its whole history is a long continual
struggle against this darkness, which has gradually melted away beneath these rays of light,
but has never entirely ceased to veil the general
trend of Russian thought.

As a result of the unfortunate circumstances
which characterize her history, Russia was for
a long time deprived of any relations with civilized Europe. The necessity of concentrating all
her strength on fighting the Mongolians laid the
corner-stone of a sort of semi-Asiatic political
autocracy. Besides, the influence of the Byzantine clergy made the nation hostile to the ideas
and science of the Occident, which were represented as heresies incompatible with the orthodox faith. However, when she finally threw off
the Mongolian yoke, and when she found herself
face to face with Europe, Russia was led to
enter into diplomatic relations with the various
Western powers. She then realized that European art and science were indispensable to her,
if only to strengthen her in warfare against
these States. For this reason a number of European ideas began to come into Russia during
the reigns of the last Muscovite sovereigns.
But they assumed a somewhat sacerdotal character in passing through the filter of Polish
society, and took on, so to speak, a dogmatic
air. In general, European influence was not

accepted in Russia except with extreme repugnance and restless circumspection, until the accession of Peter I. This great monarch, blessed with unusual intelligence and a will of iron, decided to use all his autocratic power in impressing, to use the words of Pushkin, " a new direction upon the Russian vessel; " — Europe instead of Asia.

Peter the Great had to contend against the partisans of ancient tradition, the " obscurists " and the adversaries of profane science; and this inevitable struggle determined the first character of Russian literature, where the satiric element, which in essence is an attack on the enemies of reform, predominates. In organizing grotesque processions, clownish masquerades, in which the long-skirted clothes and the streaming beards of the honorable champions of times gone by were ridiculed, Peter himself appeared as a pitiless destroyer of the ancient costumes and superannuated ideas.

The example set by the practical irony of this man was followed, soon after the death of the Tsar, by Kantemir, the first Russian author who wrote satirical verses. These verses were very much appreciated in his time. In them, he mocks with considerable fervor the ignorant contemners of science, who taste happiness only in the gratification of their material appetites.

At the same time that the Russian authors

pursued the enemies of learning with sarcasm, they heaped up eulogies, which bordered on idolatry, on Peter I, and, after him, on his successors. In these praises, which were excessively hyperbolical, there was always some sincerity. Peter had, in fact, in his reign, paved the way for European civilization, and it seemed merely to be waiting for the sovereigns, Peter's successors, to go on with the work started by their illustrious ancestor. The most powerful leaders, and the first representatives of the new literature, strode ahead, then, hand in hand, but their paths before long diverged. Peter the Great wanted to use European science for practical purposes only: it was only to help the State, to make capable generals, to win wars, to help savants find means to develop the national wealth by industry and commerce; he — Peter — had no time to think of other things. But science throws her light into the most hidden corners, and when it brings social and political iniquities to light, then the government hastens to persecute that which, up to this time, it has encouraged.

The protective, and later hostile, tendencies of the government in regard to authors manifested themselves with a special violence during the reign of Catherine II. This erudite woman, an admirer of Voltaire and of the French " encyclopédistes," was personally interested in

writing. She wrote several plays in which she
ridiculed the coarse manners and the ignorance
of the society of her time. Under the influence
of this new impulse, which had come from one
in such a high station in life, a legion of
satirical journals flooded the country. The
talented and spiritual von Vizin wrote comedies,
the most famous of which exposes the ignorance
and cruelty of country gentlemen; in another,
he shows the ridiculousness of people who take
only the brilliant outside shell from European
civilization. Shortly, Radishchev's "Voyage
from Moscow to St. Petersburg" appeared.
Here the author, with the fury of passionate
resentment, and with sad bitterness, exposes the
miserable condition of the people under the
yoke of the high and mighty. It was then that
the empress, Catherine the Great, so gentle to
the world at large and so authoritative at home,
perceiving that satire no longer spared the
guardian principles necessary for the security
of the State, any more than they did popular
superstitions, manifested a strong displeasure
against it. Consequently, the satirical journals
disappeared as quickly as they had appeared.
Von Vizin, who, in his pleasing "Questions to
Catherine" had touched on various subjects
connected with court etiquette, and on the
miseries of political life, had to content himself
with silence. Radishchev was arrested, thrown

into a fortress, and then sent to Siberia. They went so far as to accuse Derzhavin, the greatest poet of this time, the celebrated "chanter of Catherine," in his old age, of Jacobinism for having translated into verse one of the psalms of David; besides this, the energetic apostle of learning, Novikov, a journalist, a writer, and the founder of a remarkable society which devoted itself to the publication and circulation of useful books, was accused of having had relations with foreign secret societies. He was confined in the fortress at Schluesselburg after all his belongings had been confiscated. The critic and the satirist had had their wings clipped. But it was no longer possible to check this tendency, for, by force of circumstances, it had been planted in the very soul of every Russian who compared the conditions of life in his country with what European civilization had done for the neighboring countries.

Excluded from journalism, this satiric tendency took refuge in literature, where the novel and the story trace the incidents of daily life. Since the writers could not touch the evil at its source, they showed its consequences for social life. They represented with eloquence the empty and deplorable banality of the existence forced upon most of them. By expressing in various ways general aspirations towards something better, they let literature continue its teaching, even in times particularly hostile to freedom of thought, like the reign of Nicholas I, the most typical and decided adversary of the freedom of the pen that Europe has ever seen. Literature was, then, considered as an inevitable evil, but one from which the world wanted to free itself; and every man of letters seemed to be under suspicion. During this reign, not only criticisms of the government, but also praises of it, were considered offensive and out of place. Thus, the chief of the secret police, when he found that a writer of that time, Bulgarine, whose name was synonymous with accuser and like evils, had taken the liberty to praise the government for some insignificant improvements made on a certain street, told him with severity: " You are not asked to praise the government, you must only praise men of letters."

Nothing went to print without the authorization of the general censor, an authorization that had to be confirmed by the various parts of the complex machine, and, finally, by a superior committee which censored the censors. The latter were themselves so terrorized that they scented subversive ideas even in cook-books, in technical musical terms, and in punctuation marks. It would seem that under such conditions no kind of literature, and certainly no satire, could exist. Nevertheless, it was at this period that Gogol produced his best works.

The two most important are, his comedy " The
Revizor," where he stigmatizes the abuses of
administration, and " Dead Souls," that classic
work which de Vogüé judges worthy of being
given a place in universal literature, between
" Don Quixote " and " Gil Blas," and which,
in a series of immortal types, flagellates the
moral emptiness and the mediocrity of life in
high Russian society at that time.

At the same time, Griboyedov's famous
comedy, " Intelligence Comes to Grief," which
the censorship forbade to be produced or even
published, was being circulated in manuscript
form. This comedy, a veritable masterpiece,
has for its hero a man named Chatsky, who was
condemned as a madman by the aristocratic
society of Moscow on account of his independent spirit and patriotic sentiments. It is true
that in all of these works the authors hardly
attack important personages or the essential
bases of political organization. The function-
aries and proprietors of Gogol's works are
" petites gens," and the civic pathos of Chatsky
aims at certain individuals and not at the national institutions. But these attacks, cleverly
veiling the general conditions of Russian life,
led the intelligent reader to meditate on certain
questions, and it also permitted satire to live
through the most painful periods. Later, with
the coming of the reforms of Alexander II,

satire manifested itself more openly in the works of Saltykov, who was not afraid to use all his talent in scourging, with his biting sarcasm, violence and arbitrariness.

Another salient trait of Russian literature is its tendency toward realism, the germ of which can be seen even in the most old-fashioned works, when, following the precepts of the West, they were taken up first with pseudo-classicism, and then with the romantic spirit which followed.

Pseudo-classicism had but few worthy representatives in Russia, if we omit the poet Derzhavin, whom Pushkin accused of having a poor knowledge of his mother tongue, and whose monotonous work shows signs of genius only here and there.

As to romanticism! Here we find excellent translations of the German poets by Zhukovsky, and the poems of Lermontov and Pushkin, all impregnated with the spirit of Byron. But these two movements came quickly to an end. Soon realism, under the influence of Dickens and Balzac, installed itself as master of this literature, and, in spite of the repeated efforts of the symbolist schools, nothing has yet been able to wipe it out. Thus, the triumph of realism was not, as in the case of earlier tendencies, the simple result of the spirit of imitation which urges authors to choose models that are in vogue, but it was a response to a powerful instinct. The truth of this statement is very evident in view of the fact that realism appeared in Russian literature at a time when it was still a novelty in Europe. The need of representing naked reality, without any decorations, is, so to speak, innate in the Russian author, who cannot, for any length of time, be led away from this practice. This is the very reason why the Byronian influence, at the time of Pushkin and Lermontov, lasted such a short time. After having written several poems inspired by the English poet, Pushkin soon disdained this model, which was the sole object of European imitation. " Byron's characters," he says, " are not real people, but rather incarnations of the various moods of the poet," and he ends by saying that Byron is " great but monotonous." We find the same thing in Lermontov, who was fond of Byron, not only in a transient mood of snobbery, but because the very strong and sombre character of his imagination naturally led him to choose this kind of intense poetry. He was exerting himself to regard reality seriously and to reproduce it with exactitude, at the very time when he was killed in a duel at the youthful age of twenty-seven.

Pushkin's best work, his novel in verse, " Evgeny Onyegin," although it came so early, was constructed according to realistic prin-

ciples; and although we still distinguish romantic tints, it is a striking picture of Russian society at the beginning of the 19th century. We
find the same tendency in Lermontov's prose
novel, " A Hero of Our Times," in which the
hero, Pechorin, has many traits in common
with Evgeny Onyegin. This book immediately
made a deep impression. It was really nothing
more than a step taken in a new direction by its
author. But it was a step that promised much.
An absurd fatality destroyed this promise, and
hindered the poet, according to the expression
of an excellent critic of that time, from " rum-
maging with his eagle eye, among the recesses
of the world."

The works of writers of secondary rank, contemporaneous with the above mentioned, also
reveal a realistic tendency. Then appeared, to
declare it with a master's power, that genius of
a realist, of whom we have already made mention, Gogol. There was general enthusiasm;
Gogol absorbed almost the entire attention of
the public and men of letters. The great critic
and publicist Byelinsky, in particular, took it
upon himself to elaborate in his works the theories of realism; he formulated the program
about 1850 under the name of the " naturalistic
school." Thus the germs of the past had ex-
panded triumphantly in the work of Gogol, and
the way was now clear for Turgenev, Dostoyev-

sky, Tolstoy, Goncharov, Ostrovsky, and Pisemsky, who, while enlarging the range and perfecting the methods of the naturalistic school, conquered for their native literature the place which it has definitely assumed in the world.

Although we may infer that Russian realism has its roots in a special spiritual predilection, we must not nevertheless forget the historical conditions which prepared the way for it and made its logical development easy. Russian literature, called on to struggle against tremendous obstacles, could hardly have gone astray in the domain of a nebulous idealism.

The third distinctive trait of this literature is found in its democratic spirit. Most of the heroes are not titled personages; they are peasants, bourgeois, petty officials, students, and, finally, " intellectuals." This democratic taste is explained by the very constitution of Russian society.

The spirit of the literature of a nation is usually a reflection of the social class which possesses the preponderant influence from a political or economic standpoint or which is marked by the strength of its numbers. The preponderance of the upper middle class in England has impressed on all the literature of that country the seal of morality belonging to that class; while in France, where aristocracy predominated, one still feels the influence of the aristocratic traditions which are so brilliantly manifested in the pseudo-classic period of its literature. But many reasons have hindered the aristocracy and the bourgeoisie from developing in Russia. The Russian bourgeois was, for a long time, nothing but a peasant who had grown rich, while the noble was distinguished more by the number of his serfs and his authority than by his moral superiority. Deprived of independence, these two classes blended and still blend with the immense number of peasants who surround them on all sides and submerge them irresistibly, however they may wish to free themselves.

Very naturally, the first Russian authors came from the class of proprietors, rural lords, who were the most intelligent, not to say the only intelligent people. In general, the life of the lord was barely distinguishable from that of the peasant. As he was usually reared in the country, he passed his childhood among the village children; the people most dear to his heart, often more dear to him than his father or mother, were his nurse and the other servants, — simple people, who took care of him and gave him the pleasures of his youthful existence. Before he entered the local government school, he had been impregnated with goodness and popular poetry, drawn from stories, legends, and tales

to which he had been an ardent listener. We
find the great Pushkin dedicating his most
pathetic verses to his old nurse, and we often
see him inspired by the most humble people. In
this way, to the theoretic democracy imported
from Europe is united, in the case of the Russian author, a treasure of ardent personal recollections; democracy is not for him an abstract
love of the people, but a real affection, a tenderness made up of lasting reminiscences which
he feels deeply.

This then was the mental state of the most
intelligent part of this Russian nobility, which
showed itself a pioneer of the ideas of progress
in literature and life. There were even singular
political manifestations produced. Rostopchin
said: " In France the shoemakers want to become noble; while here, the nobles would like to
turn shoemakers." But, in spite of all, the
greater part of this caste, with its essential conservative instincts, was nothing more than an
inert mass, without initiative, and incapable
even of defending its own interests except by
the aid of the government.

Rostopchin did not suspect the profound
truth of his capricious saying.

This truth burst forth in all its strength
about 1870, the time of the great reforms undertaken by Alexander II, when the interests of
the people were, for the first time, the order of

the day. It was at this period that a great deal
of studying was being done with great enthusiasm and that a general infatuation for folk-
lore and for a " union with the masses " was
being shown. The desire to become " sim-
plified," that is to say to have all people live
the same kind of life, the appearance of a type,
celebrated under the sarcastic name of " noble
penitent " (meaning the titled man who is
ashamed of his privileged position as if it were
a humiliating and infamous thing), the politico-
socialistic ideology of the first Slavophiles, still
half conservative, but wholly democratic; all
these things were the results of the manifestations which astonished Rostopchin and made the
more intelligent class of Russians fraternize
more with the masses. In our day, this tendency
has been eloquently illustrated by the greatest
Russian artist and thinker, Tolstoy, who was
the very incarnation of the ideas named above,
and who always appears to us as a highly cul-
tured peasant. The hero of " Resurrection "
sums up in a few words this sympathy for the
people: " This is it, the big world, the true
world! " he says, on seeing the crowd of peasants and workingmen packed into a third-class
compartment.

In the last half of the 19th century, Russian
literature took a further step in the way of
democracy. It passed from the hands of the

nobility into the hands of the middle class, as
the conditions under which it existed brought it
closer to the people and made it therefore more
accessible to their aspirations. It is no longer
the great humanitarians of the privileged class
who paint the miserable conditions among which
people vegetate; it is the people themselves who
are beginning to speak of their miseries and of
their hopes for a better life. The result is a
deep penetration of the popular mind, in con-
junction with an acute, and sometimes sickly,
nervousness, which is shown in the works of the
great Uspensky, and, more recently still, in
Tchekoff, Andreyev, and many others.

None of these writers belong to the aristocracy, and two of them — Tchekoff and Gorky
— have come up from the masses: the former
was the son of a serf, and the latter the son of
a workingman. Let me add that, among the
women of letters, the one who is most distinguished by her talent in describing scenes from
popular life — Mme. Dmitrieva — is the
daughter of a peasant woman.

Thus, as we have shown, the Russian writers
alone, under the cover of imaginative works
which became expressive symbols, could under-
take a truly efficacious struggle against tyranny
and arbitrariness. They found themselves in
that way placed in a peculiar social position
with corresponding duties. Men expected from

them, naturally, a new gospel and also a plan of conduct necessary in order to escape from the circle of oppression. The best of the Russian writers have undertaken a difficult and perilous task; they have become the guides, and, so to speak, the "masters" of life. This tendency constitutes a new trait in Russian literature, one of its most characteristic; not that other literatures have neglected it, but no other literature in the world has proclaimed this mission with such a degree of energy and with such a spirit of sacrifice. Never, in any other country, have novelists or poets felt with such intensity the burden on their souls. At this point Gogol, first of all, became the victim of this state of things.

The enthusiasm stirred up by his works and by the immense hopes that he had evoked suddenly elevated him to such a height in the minds of his contemporaries that he felt real anguish. Artist he was, and now he forced himself to become a moralist; he rushed into philosophical speculations which led him on to a nebulous mysticism, from which his talent suffered severely. When he realized what had happened, despair seized him, his ideas troubled him, and he died in terrible intellectual distress.

We see also the great admirer of Gogol — Dostoyevsky — under different pretexts making known in almost all his novels and especially in his magazine articles, " Recollections of an Author," his opinions on the reforms about to be realized. He studies the problems of civilization which concern humanity in general, and particularly insists upon the mission of the Russian people, who are destined, he believes, to end all the conflicts of the world by virtue of a system based upon Christian love and pity.

Turgenev, himself, although above all an artist, does not remain aloof from this educational work. In his " Annals of a Sportsman," he attacks bondage. And when it was abolished, and when in the very heart of Russian society, among the younger generation, the revolutionists appeared, Turgenev attempted to paint these " new men." Thus in his novel, " Fathers and Sons," he sketches in bold strokes the character of the nihilist Bazarov. This celebrated type cannot, however, be considered a true representative of the mentality of the " new men," for it gave only a few aspects of their character, which, besides, did not have Turgenev's sympathy.

They are valued in an entirely different way by Chernyshevsky in his novel, " What Is To Be Done? " where the author, one of the most powerful representatives of the great movement toward freedom from 1860 to 1870, carefully studied the bases of the new morals and the means to be used in struggling against the prejudices of the old society. Finally let us mention Tolstoy, whose entire literary activity was a constant search for truth, till the day when his mind found an answer to his doubts in the religion of love and harmony which he preached from then on.

The earnestness which sees an apostle in a writer has not ceased to grow and has almost blinded the public.

For example, Gorky needed only to write some stories in which he places before us beings belonging to the most miserable classes of society, to be suddenly, and perhaps against his own will, elevated to the rôle of prophet of a new gospel, of annunciator from whom they were waiting for the Word, although one could also find the Word in the anti-socialistic circles which he depicts. Another contemporaneous author, Tchekoff, once wrote a story about the precarious position of the workingman in the city; he showed how this man, after he had become old and had gone back to his native village, suffered even more misery than before instead of getting the rest he had hoped for. Immediately an ardent controversy took place between the two factions of the youth of that time, the Populists and the Marxists. The former, defending the rural population, accused the author of having exaggerated and of having only superficially considered the question, while the others triumphed, confident in the activity of the people of the city.

The literary critic, however, in carefully studying the works of these authors, tried to get at the real meaning, — the idea between the lines. Gorky's philosophy has often been discussed; a great many men of letters have tried to unravel what there was of pessimism, of indifference or of mystic idealism in the soul of Tchekoff. This everlasting habit, not to say this mania, of analyzing the mind or soul of an author in order to get at his conception, his personal doctrine of life, often leads to partial and erroneous conclusions, especially when, as in most cases, the critic has only a very vague idea of the main current of thought which formed the genesis of the work.

The hopes and emotions which are aroused by every original expression in literature, show more than ever what hopes are based upon its rôle, the mission which has devolved on it to serve life, by formulating the facts of the ideal to be realized.

But what is this ideal? What are these ideal aspirations? Of what elements are they made up? What is the state of mind of the great majority of Russian " intellectuals " in the midst of the enmity which compromises and menaces them?

Thanks to the window pierced by Peter the

Great in the thick Muscovite wall, the Russian
" intellectuals " have begun to have a general
idea of European civilization. They have ad-
mired the beauty of this culture, and the great-
ness of European political and social institutions, guarantees of the dignity of human beings; they have endured mental suffering because they have found that in Russia such
independence would be impossible, and, consequently, they have had a feeling of extreme bitterness, which has forced them either to deny or
calumniate the moral forces of their country, or
to formulate very strange theories about this situation. Thus at the end of the first twenty-five
years of the century, Chadayev, one of the most
original and brilliant thinkers of Russia, developed the following thesis in his " Philosophical
Letters " : — the fatal course of history having
opposed the union of the Russian people with
Catholicism, through which European civilization developed, Russia found herself reduced
forever to the existence of an inert mass, deprived of all interior energy, as can be shown
adequately by her history, her customs, and
even the aspect of her national type with its
ill-defined traits and apathetic expression.

In the course of the terrible struggle which
he waged against the censorship and against
influential persons evilly disposed toward him,

Pushkin cried out: " It was the idea of the devil himself that made me be born in Russia! " And in one of his letters, he says, " Naturally, I despise my country from east to west, but, nevertheless, I hate to hear a stranger speak of it with scorn." Lermontov, exiled to the Caucasus, ironically takes leave of his country, which he calls, " a squalid country of slaves and masters." And he salutes the Caucasian mountains as the immense screen which may hide him from the eyes of the Russian pachas. The Slavophiles themselves, the patriots who in their way idealized both Russian orthodoxy and autocracy, and who were wrongly considered the champions of the existing order of things, showed themselves no less hostile. One of their most celebrated representatives, Khomyakov, sees in Russia " a land stigmatized " by serfdom, where all is injustice, lies, morbid laziness and turpitude.

Dostoyevsky, who shared some of the illusions of the Slavophiles, speaks of Europe as " a land of sacred miracles." Nevertheless, yielding to his desire to heighten the prestige of his country, he adds: " The Russian is not partially European, but essentially so, in the very largest sense of the word, because he watches, with an impartial love, the progress achieved by the various peoples of Europe, while each one of *them* appreciates, above all, the progress of his own country, and often does not want to let the others share it."

In spite of the seductive powers which European civilization exercised upon Russia, the Russians perceived its weak sides, which they studied by the light of the ideal which they promised themselves to attain in some indefinite future, a future which they nevertheless hoped was near at hand.

To them, enthusiastic observers that they were, these defects became more apparent than to the Europeans themselves; as their critical sense was not deadened by the wear of constant use, they saw in a clear light the inconveniences of certain institutions, they perceived the sad consequences of the excessive triumph of individualism in its struggle for life, the enfranchisement of the proletariat, the satisfaction of the few at the cost of the many. At times the bases of this civilization seemed fragile to the Russians; they had a feeling that it was not finished; they also aspired more and more to the harmonious equilibrium of society which appealed to their ideal.

In a word, that which has always been called socialism, has had an irresistible attraction for the more intelligent Russians; all of Russian literature is permeated with it, and it has developed all the more easily because it found a favorable basis in Russia's natural democracy.

During the period when this literature was
most persecuted — that is to say in the second
half of the 19th century — its most influential
representatives were ardent socialists. Among
them should be mentioned the critic Byelinsky,
the " Petracheviens," — adepts in the doctrine
of Fourier, — and that powerful agitator of
ideas, Hertzen, who founded the Russian free
press in London. Among Western writers,
there were two well liked in Russia: George
Sand and Charles Dickens. The former was a
socialist, the latter was a democrat. Their influence was very great in Russia; their works
were read with ardor, and gave rise to thoughts
which escaped the severities of the censor, but
betrayed themselves in private conversation, as
well as in certain literary circles.

All the celebrated writers of Europe who
professed liberal tendencies met with a greater
sympathy among the Russians of that time than
in their own country. Dickens, received with
great enthusiasm in Russia, was not appreciated
by the English public. His excellent translator,
Vedensky, tried hard to persuade him to come
to Russia to live, where his talents would be
valued at their true worth. We can then read-
ily understand how Dostoyevsky, in his " Memoirs of an Author," had the right to say that
the European socialistic-democrats had two
countries, first their own, then Russia.

The Russian writers who gave themselves up so passionately to this influence, — still so new even in Europe, — not able to support their political ideal, with a press, as it were, gagged by the censor, engaged in the struggle along the line of customs. They attacked the prejudices which clog the relations among men, and rose up against family despotism and the inferior position of women from a civil and economic point of view. But, between 1860 and 1870, when the enfranchisement of the serfs reduced the power of the censor, all that had been confined in the souls of the Russians burst forth. Chernishevsky wrote economic articles on capital and on the agricultural community; he studied the system of John Stuart Mill, from which he deduced his socialistic conclusions, and his reputation grew immediately at home and abroad. He became a leader of thought among the new generation.

At the same time, the young critic Dobrolyubov, author of an analytical study of Russian customs, "The Kingdom of Shadows," called the " intellectuals " to a struggle for the rights of the oppressed people, and was ready himself to " drain the bitter cup intended for those who have been sacrificed." Also at this time there appeared the poet Nekrasov and the satirist Saltykov. The former, a profound pessimist, described in his best verses the bitter fate of the lower classes; the latter with his sarcasm scathed bureaucratic arbitrariness, while from abroad was heard the free ringing of "The Bell," — a paper founded by Hertzen, — which seemed to be announcing that freedom was coming. Two articles by the poet Mikhailov on the situation of women started a vast movement. The women soon filled the lecture-halls of the university, and the class-rooms, and organized a veritable campaign to defend their rights in the name of the principle of liberty. All the partisans of democracy or socialism applauded them. The agitation became general; it seemed as if they wanted to make up for lost time by this tremendous activity; everywhere Sunday schools were started and public libraries opened; workingmen's associations were formed on socialistic principles, and the ardent younger generation spoke to the ignorant masses and asked them to join them in the coming struggle.

This epoch has been called "the moral springtime" of Russia, and in truth it was a spring with all of its real splendors and illusions. A sudden wave of life surged from one end of the empire to the other. Up above, the government was making reforms prudently, as if afraid of going too far; down below, a great transformation was taking place. It was at this time that certain bold projects were contemplated at which the government took fright. The

" springtime " proved ephemeral. A triumphant
reaction nipped in the bud this movement
towards emancipation, with all its hopes. In
1877, after the Russo-Turkish war, it seemed as
if the movement were going to start again.
Less vast and less diverse, but more definite, it
immediately put all of its strength into the
popular propaganda and showed its activity by
the assassination of the emperor and by several
other crimes. It was a terrible struggle, till
finally the leaders again succumbed under the
mighty blows of their adversaries. The years
that followed this defeat (1880-1905) were most
inauspicious in Russian life. A profound
apathy deadened society, and an atmosphere
of anguish and disillusion — which have left
visible traces in Russian literature — weighed
it down.

In short, it may be said that Russian thought
has always been led away by the theories of
certain European parties who are most opposed
to political and social organization of the state.
The vigor, the clearness, and the force of
negation with which this characteristic manifests
itself in the ideas and customs of the Russian
radical-socialists have often distorted, in the
eyes of other countries, opinions or doctrines
which it is important to present in their true
light.

Thus, Bazarov, that nihilistic creation of Turgenev, appeared to the English, French, and German public as a mystical hero not viable in human society, while Pisarev, one of the sanest of Russian critics, considers him as a model of the really free man. As to Turgenev himself, he saw that the coming of this type would make concrete a rising force worthy of holding attention and also of commanding some respect.

In practical life, this negative force has found its most extreme expression in what has already been pointed out, that is, in the revolutionary anarchism of Bakunin and in Tolstoy's recent theories of pacific anarchism, which are founded on the gospel. But, while very significant as great illustrations of certain sides of Russian mentality, neither the one nor the other of these anarchistic doctrines, so opposed in their substance, can be considered as an expression of the modern Russian socialistic movement. Having found a basis in the workingman movement of their country, the Russian socialistic theoreticians have become more practical, and their activity turns back to the realm of European socialism, which is to be found in the doctrines of Karl Marx.

There was a time in Europe when they christened with the name " nihilism " this active negation of civilization and of bourgeois cus-

toms, so characteristic of the Russian " intellectuals." Taken in its literal sense, this word
is inexact, since those to whom it was applied
were inspired by a very high ideal. In a loose
use of the word, nihilism has, on the contrary,
a real significance, especially if one connects it
with most of the Russian " intellectuals." The
liberal tendencies which were brewing in the
realistic literature of the period from 1840 to
1850, and which manifested themselves suddenly
with particular strength during the tumultuous
decade between 1860 and 1870, made the substance of the new theories and the base of Russian mentality. These theories were very bold
in their negation, and it is for this reason that
they have been called " nihilistic."

If this intellectual " élite " should some day
triumph in Russia, will it be true to its moral
idea of justice and liberty? It probably will.
We may then see the following phenomenon take
place: the realization of the most advanced program of modern civilization in one of the most
backward countries of Europe.

However paradoxical such a prevision may
seem at first, it has a fundamental element of
truth. Two obstacles bar the way to civilization
and the normal development of new ideas, which
are the foundation of progress. First of all,
there is the naïve and boorish ignorance of the
common people; then the resistance which every

established society instinctively offers to ideas
of reformation.   Of these two conservative
forces, Russia knows but one, pure and simple
ignorance, while the second, which can have art
and science as powerful allies, is completely lacking.   But ignorance cannot last forever.   It
diminishes more and more; that is why the most
advanced ideas of European civilization naturally go hand in hand with learning in Russia,
and occupy all places which knowledge wins
from ignorance.   Since the Russian has had a
taste of science he has become the champion of
social and democratic ideas; the latter develop
even with elementary instruction, as can easily
be seen by observing the movements made among
the workmen of the city, and also among the
more advanced elements of the peasant population.

These particulars had already attracted the
attention of the brilliant peace advocate and
profound thinker, Hertzen, who, distressed by
the bloody reprisals of bourgeoise Europe,
following the Revolution of 1848, fixed his attention on Russia, from which he expected great
things, — among others, a new civilization freed
from the prejudices and customs which held it
back in other countries.

Hertzen represented Russia as an immense
plain where people were getting rid of old
thatched cottages, and at the same time collect-

ing the necessary materials for new habitations.
He saw a world in which no one lived as yet, but
where life as it should be was being prepared for.
And this idea, which may seem exaggerated, has
a good deal of sense in it. Does not every backward nation, which hastens to take her place in
the circle of the more advanced peoples of Europe, resemble a vessel into which a new wine is
to be poured?

If modern Russian literature has not deviated
from its fundamental principles, realism, democracy, and socialism, on the other hand, a radical
change has taken place in society which has
necessarily had an influence on it. The popu-
lace is not the sombre, inert, and ignorant multitude that it has been heretofore. Learning is
penetrating more and more; and as an advance-
guard, it has the workingmen of the city and
the people of the suburbs. A feeling of dignity,
of human personality, and a love of liberty is
awakening in the masses who have joined in the
struggle which the " intellectuals " are conduct-
ing against the passive forces of autocracy.

That is why the literature of this time — always excepting the period from 1905 to 1910
— is preëminently a literature of fiercer and
more active combat than ever before. As in
times gone by, the heroes of this literature are
common people. The writers choose them from

among the students, schoolmasters, and school-
mistresses of the village schools, who with complete disregard of self carry on the great work
of popular education in the very heart of the
country, without caring about the arbitrary
power which menaces them, or the moral and
material conditions of their lives. They also
choose them from among the doctors of the districts who are worn out in despairing efforts to
struggle against the terrible epidemics, and who
are also trying to improve hygienic conditions
among the peasants. In fine, among the heroes
are included all who sacrifice their personal interests for the general good.

The results of this terrible struggle against
brute force are shown in the excessive nervousness of the combatants, who have become delirious with their aspirations towards liberty.
Hatred of actual reality and distrust of those
who have resigned themselves to it have made
them accept sympathetically the most extreme
and uncompromising measures, and one often
thinks one sees a certain generosity among the
people who are at war with society, — often, it
is true, for egotistical reasons, far removed from
the great ideal of reforms profitable to the
masses. Such are the celebrated barefoot
brigade, the eternal vagabonds, the " lumpen-
proletariat " of Gorky's early works.

Another favorite subject of the Russian au-

thors is the antagonism which makes parents
and children quarrel. But the children who were
radicals of the former generation have now became fathers, and are often reproached by their
sons for the practical impossibility of the ideal
for which they vainly expended their strength,
and, as a result of which, they are worn out and
useless. Veressayev and Chirikov have written
most on this point.

However, in spite of repeated attacks, the resistance has grown in intensity and the general
uneasiness has spread without any one's being
able as yet to see any lasting or positive result.
The pessimism of various writers faithfully reflects this crisis. Andreyev, for instance, possesses an extraordinary intuition of the element
of tragic mysteriousness which envelops the
slightest circumstances of daily life. Tchekoff,
the prominent author who died a few years ago,
has left us remarkably realistic sketches, where
he obviously shows mental discouragement as a
result of the struggle. Another contemporary
writer, Korolenko, whose poetic talent recalls
Turgenev to our minds, is distinguished, on the
contrary, by the attempts he has made to set
free the spark of life which exists in human beings who have broken down morally. All these
writers have such a direct and powerful influence
on contemporary youth that we are going to
study them separately in this book, not except-

ing Tchekoff, whose influence is still enormous.

Since the death of the prophet of Yasnaya-Polyana,[1] Russian literature cannot boast of any writers who compare with Turgenev, Dostoyevsky, Goncharov, or the dramatist Ostrovsky. The cause is to be traced rather to circumstances than to the authors themselves. For social life to furnish material suitable for the artist's description, it must first of all have types which show a certain consistency, a more or less determined attitude. But it is futile to look for either stability or precision in Russian life since Russia has been going through continual crises. It would be just as difficult for literature to record rapid changes of ideas, as for an artist to copy a model that cannot pose for him. Besides, most contemporary writers are struggling hard for the means of subsistence.

Sometimes their effort to get food has so sapped their strength that they have not had enough time to finish their studies, nor enough tranquillity of soul to apply their talents to an impartial view of life and to incorporating in their work the documents which they have collected. Even in the writing of the best Russian authors of to-day one often feels that there is something unfinished, or hasty, as if their thoughts had not matured.

I do not think that it will be superfluous to add that all Russian literature for the past century has been able to express only a very small part of what it had to say. The Russian writer continually suffers from the constraint which forces him to check the flight of his inspiration in order to escape from the foolish and often stupid sternness of the pitiless censor. The poet Nekrasov shows us in one of his poems an old soldier who has become a printer, and who speaks in the following manner of Pushkin:

"He was a good man, tipped very generously, but he never ceased to rage against the censor. When he saw his manuscripts marked with red crosses, he became furious. One day, in order to console him, I said:

"'Bah! why torment yourself?'

"'Why,' he cried, 'but it is blood that is flowing, — blood, — my blood!'"

A great deal of blood was thus shed. And in order to accentuate the action of the censor the police dealt cruel blows to the authors. One day Pushkin was called to the head of the department. They believed that they had recognized in one of his satires a certain gentleman, named N. G., who demanded that Pushkin be severely punished. Unnerved by the cross-examination to which he was put, the poet cried:

"But it isn't N. G. whom I have drawn!"

"Who is it, then?"

" It is you, yourself," replied the poet.

" That is madness, sir," the high dignitary cried out with wrath. " You say that wood belonging to the state was stolen. And at the time when these thefts were committed I was away."

" Then you do not recognize yourself in my satire? "

" No, a thousand times no! "

" And N. G. recognizes himself? "

" Not exactly, but as he is in the service of the government . . ."

" Well, is he its spokesman and champion? And why is it precisely he who asks to have me arrested? "

" All right," replied the dignitary, suddenly becoming milder, " I shall inform His Majesty of our conversation."

The affair ended without further complications. It should be noted that the Tsar himself protected Pushkin, for Pushkin had got into touch with him in order to influence him more successfully. Nevertheless, this acquaintance was only a new source of suffering to the poet. In the case of certain less known writers the malevolence of the higher authorities often took on a tragic turn. For a single poem in which the poet Polezhayev described a students' debauch, the author was reduced by Nicholas I to the rank of a common soldier. Sokolovsky, an-

other writer of this time, not being able to get
a footing in literature, abandoned the pen, and
like many others, sought to forget his disap-
pointment in drink. For several years Hertzen
was transferred from one place of exile to another until he came to England. And how terrible was the fate of the talented poet of Little
Russia, Shevchenko, who was exiled for many
years to a corner of European Russia and forbidden to do any writing or even painting, a
thing that he loved above all! And finally, who
does not know the sad comedy of Dostoyevsky,
who was made to go through all the prepara-
tions for his execution, but was finally sent to
that prison which he has so wonderfully described in his recollections of " The Dead
House "?

The Damocles' sword of defiant authority was
suspended over the head of every Russian writer.
The vocation of literature was filled with danger
and brought about actual tragedies in some
families. Thus, Pushkin's father, fearing that
the fury of the authorities would extend to him,
began to hate all literature, and had serious
quarrels with his son. Griboyedov's mother
threw herself at her son's feet and begged him
not to write any more but rather to enter the
service of the State. In Griboyedov we have a
sad example of a great talent virtually buried
alive by the censor. His comedy, " Intelligence

Comes to Grief," is a masterful work, sparkling
with satiric warmth, the equal of which it would
be hard to find anywhere. This first work, rich
in promise, was never published nor produced.
Discouraged, the author renounced literature,
and on the advice of his mother, accepted a position as ambassador to Persia, where he was
killed in a riot.

Not only does the censorship mutilate literary works, but it often suffocates the inspiration of the author. The Russian press has lately
published a very interesting article on Nekrasov,
explaining the frequent interruptions of his
activity by a momentary paralysis of his inspiration. Often, he writes, the ideas and
poetic forms which come to his mind are so
strong that he need only take up his pen and
write them down. But the thought that what
he might write would be condemned by the
censor, stops him. It was, then, a long struggle
between the ideas which he wanted to express
and the obstacles which hindered him. And
when finally Nekrasov had smothered his inspiration, he was broken down and crushed by
fatigue and disgust, and for a long time he
stopped writing. His friends advised him to
jot down his ideas in spite of all, in the hope
that they would be recognized by future generations when happier days should dawn on

literature. He was not successful, because in order to create his genius needed to feel a close bond between him and his readers. Thus the censor carried his brutal hand into the very laboratory of thought.

Happily, since the movement toward reform between 1860 and 1870, the Russian censor has become more lenient and now no one says what was once said to the writer Bulgarin: " Your business is to describe public activities, popular holidays, the theatre. Do not look for other topics." The number of subjects open to the press has increased. But the desire to live a free life has developed in literature and in society alike, and as resistance to it has also strengthened, the pressure has remained relatively the same. The censor and the police continue to stifle the natural richness and the power of the Russian mind. To-day, as before, Russian literature is made up of just that small fraction of the whole which has escaped government inquisition.

However, in spite of all the unheard-of constraints which weigh upon her, Russia has already given us such great authors, that we need not hesitate to say that on the day when she regains liberty of speech and of pen, her literature will take its place among the first in the world.

II

ANTON TCHEKOFF [2]

" There is a saying that man needs only six feet of ground, but that is for a corpse and not for a living man. It is not six feet of ground that man requires, not even an entire estate, but the whole terrestrial globe, nature in its fullness, so that all his faculties can expand freely."

This is the proud profession of faith that Anton Tchekoff made on entering the literary world. He was born January 17, 1860, at Taganrog, where his father, a freed serf, lived. After attending school in his native town, he took up the study of medicine at Moscow. Once a doctor, rather than practise, he devoted most of his time to literature. His career as an author does not offer us any extraordinary situations. He owed his success, and later on his glory, to severe and prolonged work. His literary talent manifested itself while he was still a student. He began his career with humorous short stories which were published in various newspapers. They brought him enough for the bare necessities of life.

40

These stories have been collected in two volumes. They are very short, almost miniatures. For the most part they are elegant trifles, worked out with painstaking care. One feels that the author had no definite goal in sight; he wrote them simply to amuse and entertain his readers. One would search in vain for any sort of philosophy. On the contrary, one finds there a rather significant spirit, a gaiety, care-free, loquacious and, at times, ironical. Unimportant people tell pleasant things about themselves or others. All these men are a trifle debauched, talky, futile, and their companions are flighty, intriguing little women who chatter incessantly. Everything begins and ends with a laugh. This recalls some of the early works of Gogol, but, we repeat, one finds no moral element in this laughter, and these tiny comedies are in reality no more than simple vaudeville sketches. Once in a while we find a sad note; less frequently, we find the sadness accentuated in order to present a terrible drama. Such, then, are the contents of the first two volumes which came from the pen of Tchekoff.

However, this melancholy little note, met from time to time, gradually grew in intensity in the third volume, until later on it lost all trace of the old carelessness, and developed, on the contrary, into a profound sadness. Tche-

koff unconsciously gave up the " genre " of
pleasant anecdote in order to concentrate all
his attention on facts. This practice made him
sad. Russia was, at this time, going through
a period of prostration as a result of the last
Russo-Turkish war. This war, which, at the
cost of enormous sacrifices, ended in the libera-
tion of the Bulgarian people, awakened among
the Russians a hope of obtaining their own
liberty, and provoked among the younger generation the most energetic efforts to obtain this
liberty, no matter what the cost might be.
Alas, this hope was frustrated! All efforts
were in vain, a reaction followed, and the year
1880 brought the reaction to its height.
From then on apathy followed in the steps
of the great enthusiasm. All illusion fled. A
kind of disenchantment filled all minds.
Those who had hoped with such ardor, and
had counted on their own strength, felt weak
and powerless. Some confined themselves to
moaning incessantly. A grey twilight enveloped Russian life and filled it with melancholy.
These are the dreary aspects that Tchekoff
describes, and none has excelled him in portraying the events of this hopeless reaction.
His stories and dramas give us a long procession of people who succumb to the monotony,
to the platitudes, to the desolation, of existence.

It is in the following manner that one of his characters expresses his ideas on the subject of this moral crisis:

" I was then not more than twenty-six years of age; nevertheless I was conscious not only that life was senseless, but that it was without any visible goal; that all was illusion and dupery; that, in its consequences and even in its very essence, the life of the exiled on the island of Sakhaline was very much the same as the life that was led at Nice; that the difference between the brain of Kant and the brain of a fly was very small; finally, that no one in this world was either right or wrong."

This idea of the nothingness of life, with its extremes, monstrous and profitless, is often found in the work of Tchekoff. His story " The Kiss " is but a variation of this theme, — the absurdity of life. Lieutenant Riabovich, under the influence of a chance kiss, a kiss that was not meant for him, dreams of love for an entire summer; he waits impatiently for the return of the pretty stranger; but alas, his lovely dream cannot be realized, for the simple and cruel reason that no one is waiting for *him*, no one is interested in him. One day, on the banks of a stream, the young officer gives himself up to his reflections:

" The water flows off; one knows not where nor why; it flowed in exactly the same way

last May; from the stream it flows into the
river, and then into the sea; then it evaporates,
turns into rain, and perhaps the very same
water again flows by before my eyes. . . . To
what good? Why?" And all life appears to
Riabovich an absurd mystification and seems
thoroughly senseless.

The hero of "The Bet" absolutely scorns
humanity, with its petty and its great deeds,
its little and its great ideas, because he feels
that after all everything must disappear, be
annihilated, and the earth itself will turn into
a mass of ice.

Tchekoff has given us innumerable rough
sketches typical of people belonging to the
most diverse social classes. He seems to take
his readers by the hand and to lead them
wherever he can show them characteristic scenes
of modern Russian society, — be it in the country, in the factory, in princely dwellings, at the
post-office, or on the highway. He barely takes
the time absolutely necessary to depict in a
few, appropriate words a state of mind or the
secret of a gesture. One would say that he
hastens to express the totality of life with the
variety of his detached manifestations of it.
That is why his stories are short; often mere
allusions stand in place of actual development.
And whatever domains or corners of Russian

life the reader, under the guiding hand of this perspicacious cicerone, may visit, he will almost always go away with one predominating impression: the lamentable isolation of Russia.

" The Windswept Grain " shows the reader a religious establishment, where a young Jew, recently converted, has taken refuge. Here is a young man, very impressionable and eager to learn, who has fled from his home and his family, whose prejudices offended him. His family tries every means to bring him back and to punish his apostasy.

In order to employ his energies effectively, the young proselyte, who has embraced the new religion only that he may follow progress, tries to get a position as a school-teacher. But the apostleship of learning cannot satisfy his versatile mind: he continues to flit from one thing to another, like a gypsophilia, driven by the wind across the entire stretch of the steppes of southern Russia.

Then Tchekoff takes us to a postal station to show us another type of the " Windswept Grain." This man, like the young convert, is a dreamer, who puts heart and soul into any new idea that comes along. He also has spent his life in searching for an activity corresponding to his ideal. At present, being a widower, he is obliged to support both himself and his daughter, who, while loving him devotedly, never ceases to reproach him for the many inconveniences of their uncertain existence. In the evening, a young widow from a neighboring province gets off at the place where he and his daughter are living. When she sees the young girl pouting, she consoles her by caressing her with the tact peculiar to women. Then, at tea time, she starts talking to the father. The idealist tells of his life, and reveals to the young woman the plans that he has made. The true sympathy with which she listens, and the respectful and tender feeling that he has for, her, inevitably makes the reader think that fate has not brought these two people together in vain, and that their lives will be united. This impression persists when on the next day we find the young woman entering her carriage assisted by her companion of the evening before. We wait for the word that will unite this couple. But neither of them pronounces the all-important phrase. The carriage leaves; the man remains for a long time motionless as a statue, watching with a mingled feeling of joy and suffering the distant road and his disappearing happiness, which, but a moment ago, he seemed to hold in his hand.

After those who insist on always realizing their temporary ideals, let us take up characters of a new type, those whom destiny has

irredeemably conquered, and who have finally
resigned themselves to their fate.

An example of this type is Sofia Lvovna in
" Volodia the Great and Volodia the Small."
Married to a rich colonel, she has no other end
in life. The days pass, tiresome, monotonous,
filled only with visits and driving; the nights
are interminable and sad near this husband whom
she does not love, and whom she married out of
spite and for money. Love for a comrade of
her youth, Volodia by name, fills her heart.
But this young man, who has recently finished
his studies, is just as commonplace and just as
debauched as her husband and the society which
surrounds her. Sofia Lvovna is not yet resigned to her fate. She speaks of her aspirations to her childhood friend, who, after getting
from her what he desires, leaves her at the end
of a week. And Sofia Lvovna becomes frightened at the thought that for the young girls
and women of her station there is no other
alternative than to go on riding in carriages,
or to enter a convent and gain salvation.

" The Attack " gives us an example of the
terrible feeling of terror that suddenly enters
the proud soul of a young man at his first contact with certain realities.

The student Vassiliev, a young man of excessively nervous temperament, has visited a
house of ill-fame, and since then, he cannot rid

himself of his painful impressions. Sombre
thoughts beset his mind: "Women, living
women!" he repeats, his head between his hands.
"If I broke this lamp you would say that it
was too bad; but down there it is not lamps
that they break, it is the existence of human
creatures! Living women! . . ."

He dreams of several ways of saving these
unfortunates, and he decides childishly to
stand on a street-corner, and say to each
passer-by:

"Where are you going? and why? Fear
God."

But this desire soon gives place to a general
state of anguish and hatred of himself. The
evil seems too great for him, and its vastness
crushes him. In the meantime, the people
about him do not suffer; they are indifferent
or incredulous. The student feels that he is
losing his mind. They confine him. Later on,
when, cured, he leaves the alienist, "he blushes
at his anxiety." . . . The general indifference
has broken down his aspirations, smothered his
vague dream.

In "Peter the Bishop," we see a man, good
and simple, the son of peasants. This man,
thanks to his intelligence, has raised himself
to the rank of bishop. During all his life he
has suffocated in this high ecclesiastical position, the pompous tinsel of which troubles him

to such an extent that the cordial and sincere relationship existing between him and his old mother, who is so full of respect for her son, is broken off. After his death he is quickly forgotten. The old mother, now childless, when she walks in the fields with the women of the village, still speaks of her children, of her grandchildren, and of her son, the bishop. But she speaks timidly of him, as if she feared that they would not believe her. And, in truth, no one puts any faith in what she says.

It is among the people and the working classes that man is most completely rid of all traces of an artificial and untruthful exterior; the struggle against misery does not leave much room for other preoccupations; life is merciless, it crushes unrelentingly man's dreams of happiness, and often does not leave any one to share the burden of sorrows or even its simple cares. The short and very touching story of " The Coachman " gives us an excellent example of this loneliness. Yona, a poor coachman, has lost his son; he feels that he has not the strength to live through this sorrow alone; he feels the absolute need of speaking to some one. But he tries in vain to confide his sorrows to one or the other of his patrons. No one listens to him. Therefore, once his day's work is over, alone in the stable, he pours out his heart to his horse: " Yes, my little mare, he is dead, my beloved child. . . . Let us suppose that you had a colt, and that this colt should suddenly die, wouldn't that cause you sorrow? " The mare looks at him with shining eyes, and snuffles the hand of her master, who ends by telling her the entire story of the sickness and death of his son.

In " The Dreams," a miserable vagabond, whom two constables are taking to the neighboring city, dreams aloud of the pleasant life he expects to lead in Siberia, whither he hopes to be deported. His gaolers listen to him not without a certain interest. They also begin to dream . . . they dream of a free country, from which they are separated by an enormous stretch of land, a country that they can hardly conceive. One of them brusquely interrupts the dreams of the vagabond: " That's all right, brother, you'll never get to that enchanted land. How are you going to get there? You are going to travel 300 versts and then you'll give your soul up to God. You are already almost gone." And then, in the imagination of the vagabond, other scenes present themselves: the slowness of justice, the temporary jails, the prison, the forced marches and the weary halts, the hard winters, sickness, the death of comrades. . . . " A shudder passes through his whole body, his head trembles and his body contracts like a worm which has been trodden upon. . . ."

Let us now look at those numerous stories of Tchekoff which treat of peasant life: " The Peasants," " The Murder," " In the Ravine," and others.

" The Peasants " is one of the most important of the stories which treat of the country, and was recently conspicuous for bringing up the question, violently discussed by the Marxists and the Populists, of the life of the people in the city and in the country.

Nicholas Chigueldyev, a waiter in a Moscow hotel, falls sick and has to leave his work. All his savings go into the hands of the doctor and the druggist. As he does not seem to improve, he decides to return to his native village, where his family is still living. If the air of the country does not cure him, he will at least die at home. He had left the village at an early age, and had never gone back to visit. He goes home with his wife and his little daughter. There he finds his mother, his father, and his two brothers and their wives in the most abject misery. The whole family is entombed in a dark and filthy " isba " full of flies. Nicholas and his wife immediately see that it would have been better for them to have remained in Moscow. But it is too late. They haven't enough money to return; they must remain. A hor-

rible life begins for the sick man and his family.
There are endless quarrels, blows, abuses.
They reproach one another for eating and even
for living. They are angry at Nicholas and
his wife for having come. The latter is soon
tired of this existence. In the city Nicholas
had broken himself of country manners. He
wants to go back to Moscow. But where find
the money for the trip? . . . His sickness becomes more acute. An old tailor, a former
nurse, who has been called in, promises to cure
him; he bleeds him several times and Nicholas
dies. The widow and her little daughter spend
the winter in the village. The young woman,
who had watched during those long days of
suffering, is now broken down. When spring
comes, the mother and daughter go to the
church, and, after praying at the grave of
their dead, they go begging on the highway.

In " The Murder " Tchekoff studies certain
manifestations in the spiritual life of the
peasants. Matvey Terekof belongs to a peasant family the members of which are all
known for their piety; in the village they are
called "the singing boys." Very orthodox,
they hold themselves aloof and give themselves
over to mysticism.

Instead of playing with his little comrades,
Matvey is constantly poring over the Gospel.
His piety increases, he prays night and day,

hardly eats anything, and experiences " a singular joy at feeling himself grow weaker through the fasting." One day he notices that the priest of the village is less pious than he. He enters a convent in the hopes of finding there true Christians. But even there his disillusionment comes soon. Finally, he decides to found a church of his own. He hires a little room which he transforms into a chapel. He finds disciples and soon gains a reputation as a thaumaturgical saint.

A sect, of which he is to be the head, is in process of formation, when, one day, he finds that he is on the wrong track. He thinks he has committed a mortal sin. Pride has taken possession of him; it is the Devil and not God who now directs his moves. Conscious of his error, he returns to orthodoxy, and, in the hopes of expiating his wrong-doing, he humiliates himself everywhere and on every occasion.

But his cousin Jacob, having become infected with his earlier ideas, practises them with the fanatic ardor of a neophyte. With his sister and several other religious people, he locks himself into his house to pray; he sings vespers and matins. In the meanwhile Matvey decides that he must read Jacob a sermon.

" Be reasonable," he tells him repeatedly, " repent, cousin. You will lose, because you are the prey of the demon. Repent."

Instead of repenting, Jacob and his sister
vow an implacable hatred against Matvey; so
extreme is their feeling, that one day, at the
end of an altercation, Jacob, blinded by rage,
kills his cousin.

He is judged and condemned. He is sent to
the island of Sakhaline. There, he languishes,
suffers, and despairs. But, little by little, his
mind grows peaceful, and he has consoling
visions. In prison he is surrounded by pariahs
and criminals, and the sight of all this human
suffering turns him again towards God, towards
the religion of Love, the religion of pity for
mankind. And now he wants to return to the
country to tell of the miracle that has taken
place in him, and to save souls from ill and
ignorance.

In " The Ravine " evil and injustice triumph
at times with revolting cynicism. Evil is in
everything and everywhere: " in the great
manufacturers who drive along the streets of
the village, crushing men and beasts; in the
bailiff and the recorder, who are such bad characters that their very faces betray their knavery; " and finally, in the central figure of the
story, Axinia, the wife of Stepan, the youngest
son of Tzibukine, a usurer and monopolist.

The unhealthy ravine hides a village inhabited by factory workers. The best house belongs to Gregory Tzibukine, who traffics in

everything: brandy, wheat, cattle, lumber, and usury, on the side. His eldest son, Anissme, is employed at the police station and seldom comes home; the second son, Stepan, is deaf and sickly; he helps his father both well and badly, and his wife, the pretty and coquettish Axinia, runs all day between the cellar and the shop. The father Tzibukine is also friendly to her and respects this young woman, for she is a very good worker and is most intelligent. Tzibukine, a widower, has married Varvara, an affable and pious soul who gives alms, — a strange thing in this family who cheat everybody. Anissme often sends home beautiful letters and presents. One day, he comes unexpectedly; he has an unquiet, and, at the same time, flippant air. His parents have decided to get him married, and, although he is a drunkard, ugly and vulgar, they have found him a pretty wife. The girl is Lipa, daughter of a poor widow, a laborer like her mother. Anissme whistles and looks at the ceiling, and shows no signs of pleasure at his coming marriage. He leaves the house in a strange manner, and appears again three days before the wedding, bringing to his parents, as gifts, some newly coined money. The wedding day has come. The clergy and the well-to-do of the neighborhood are present at the dinner, which is sumptuously served. Lipa seems petrified with fear, for she barely knows her husband. The festivities last a long time; at intervals the voices of women can be heard outside hurling curses at the usurer. Then Anissme, red, drunk, and sweating, is shoved into the room where Lipa has already disrobed. Five days later, Anissme comes to his mother and bids her good-bye. He confides in her that some one has given him advice, and that he has decided either to become rich or to perish. Now that her husband has departed, Lipa again becomes gay.

Meanwhile, they have arrested a reaper accused of having circulated a bad piece of money which he says he received from Anissme the night of the wedding. Tzibukine goes home, examines the money that his son has given him, and decides that it is all counterfeit. He orders Axinia to throw every bit of it into the well. But, instead of obeying, she pays it out as wages to the workmen. A week passes; they find out that Anissme has been thrown into prison as a counterfeiter. Tzibukine despairs; he feels his strength diminishing. Varvara continues to pray and to watch, while Stepan and Axinia continue to ply their trade as before. When, later on, Anissme is sentenced to ten years at hard labor in Siberia, Varvara suggests to her husband that he should leave one of his houses to the child which has just been born to Lipa, so that no one will speak badly of him after his death. But, at this suggestion, Axinia flies into such a fury, that, in her homicidal rage, she throws a kettle of boiling water over the child, who dies later at the hospital. Finally, she drives the young woman out of the house. Lipa returns to her mother. Soon Axinia reigns as absolute mistress of the house. Tzibukine becomes distracted; he does not take care of his money any more, because he cannot tell the good from the bad. Rumor has it that his daughter-in-law is letting him die of hunger. Varvara still goes on with her good work. Anissme is forgotten. The old man, starving, and driven from home, lodges a complaint against the young woman. Coming back to the village, the old man, tottering along the street, meets Lipa and her mother, who are now doing tile work.

" Both bow deeply to him, and he looks at them with tears in his eyes. Lipa offers him a piece of oatmeal cake, and the two women go on their way, crossing themselves several times. . . ."

The virtuous Varvara is an extremely characteristic type, with a subtle psychology, carefully worked out; her honesty and goodness form an indispensable contrast to the ambient horrors.

The author himself explains the rôle of Var-

vara and her action in this system of evil.
" Her alms seem to be something strange, joyous and free, like the red flowers and the lights
that glow before the saintly images."   On holidays, and on jubilees, which last three days,
when coarse and rotten meat is sold to the peasants who come to pawn their scythes and hats,
or their wives' shawls; when the workingmen
lie in the gutter under the influence of bad
brandy, then " one feels a bit relieved at the
thought that down there, in that house, there
is a good and quiet woman, always ready to help
unfortunates."

Lipa and her mother are good and timid souls
who suffer in silence, and give to the poor the
little that they possess:

" It seemed to them that some one up on
high, further up than the azure, there among
the stars, saw what was going on in their village, and watched.   Big as the evil is, in spite
of it, the night is beautiful and calm; justice
is and will be calm and beautiful on God's earth
also; the universe awaits the moment when it
can melt into this justice, as the light of the
moon melts into the night."

These, then, are Tchekoff's favorite themes,
on which he has traced numerous variations, always breathing forth a profound melancholy.

" The life of our industrial classes," he says,

" is dark, and drags itself along in sort of a twilight; as to the life of our common people, workingmen and peasants, it is a black night, made up of ignorance, poverty, and all sorts of prejudices."

But from this ocean of ignorance, of barbarity, of misery which makes up the life of a peasant, Tchekoff has taken out the things of most importance, things that always happen in the most solemn moments of their existence.

" All," he says, in describing a religious procession in the country, " the old man, his wife and the others, all stretch forth their hands to the ikon of the holy Virgin, regard her ardently, and say through their tears: ' Protectress! Virgin protectress!' And all seem to have understood that the space between Heaven and Earth is not empty; that the rich and the mighty have not swallowed up everything; that there is protection against all wrongs, slavery, misery, the fatal brandy. . . ."

Besides, in a story entitled " My Life," Poloznev, speaking of the peasants, expresses himself in the following manner:

" They were, for the most part, nervous and irritable people, ignorant, and improvident, who could think of nothing but the grey earth and black bread; a people who were crafty, but were stupid about it, like the birds, who, when they want to hide themselves, only hide

their heads. They would not do the mowing
for you for twenty rubles, but they would do it
for six liters of brandy, notwithstanding the
fact that with twenty rubles they can buy eight
times as much. What vice and foolishness!
Nevertheless, one feels that the life of the
peasant has a great deal of depth. It makes no
difference that he, behind his plough, resembles
an awkward beast, or that he gets intoxicated.
In spite of all, when you look at him closely,
you feel that he possesses the essential thing,
the sentiment of justice."

This love of justice Tchekoff has had occasion to observe even among convicts. "The
convict," he says, in his book on the prison of
Sakhaline, of which he made a profound study
during his stay on the island, "the prisoner,
completely corrupted and unjust as he himself
is, loves justice more than any one else does,
and if he does not find it in his superiors, he
becomes angry, and grows baser and more dis-
trustful from year to year."

In the last works of Tchekoff the pessimistic
tendency grows greater and greater. It seems
as if the writer had gone through a sort of
moral crisis, brought on by the conflict of his
old despair and his new hopes. At this time,
Russian society itself began to shake off its
apathy, and this awakening, sweeping like a

vivifying wave into the soul of the sad artist, opened for him, at the same time, perspectives of new ideas.

This second aspect of Tchekoff's talent is perceptible in the story called " The Student." A seminarist, Velikopolsky by name, tells the gardener Vassilissa and her daughter Lukeria about St. Peter's denial of Christ. As a result of the impression which this story makes on her Vassilissa suddenly breaks into tears; she weeps a long time and hides her face as if she were ashamed of crying. Lukeria, who has been watching the student fixedly, blushes and her face takes on the tender and sad expression which is characteristic of those whose life is made up of deep suffering. After taking leave of them, the student thinks that Vassilissa's tears and the emotion of her daughter come from sorrows connected with the things he has just told them.

" If the old woman wept, it was not because he knew how to tell the story in a touching manner, but because Peter was near to her, and because she was interested, heart and soul, in what was going on in the mind of the apostle. . . ."

Joy suddenly fills his heart, and he stops a moment to take a long breath. " The past," he muses, " is bound to the present by an uninterrupted chain of events." " And it seems

to him that he has just seen the two ends of
this chain: he has touched one, and the other
has vibrated. . . ."

In an ironical manner and by using very
personal material, Tchekoff paints more than
anything else, life in its passive or negative
manifestations.   Nevertheless, it is not satire,
at least not in its general trend, for in his work
we find too much human tenderness for satire.
He does not laugh at his characters, and does
not nail them to the pillory in an outburst of
indignation.   In his writing, the fundamental
idea is fused with the form; his talent is calm,
thoughtful, observing; but it seems, at times,
that this calmness, this seeming indifference, is
only a mask.   A critic, speaking of Tchekoff,
has said: " He is a tender crayon."   It would
be hard to find a more suitable expression.
The delicacy of tone, the softness of touch in
the outlines, the polish of some of the details,
the capricious incompleteness of others are, in
fact, the mark of his talent.

Tchekoff was such a voluminous author that
it would require a veritable effort to remember
the throng of characters which exists in his
books; and it is more than difficult not to con-
fuse their individual doings and achievements.
This abundance is connected with a peculiarity
in the author's talent.   He does not exhaust his

subject; the psychology of his characters is emphasized by two or three expressive traits only, and this epitome is enough to make the theme of a story, the simplicity and naturalness of which demand, nevertheless, a high degree of art. The author is not interested in outlining the details, but the picture that he has sparingly conjured up stands out lifelike; he is always in a hurry to observe and to tell. Therefore the brevity and quantity of his stories. His stories seldom exceed ten pages in length, while some do not exceed four. They constitute a series of sketches, of miniatures of rare value, among which can be found some real gems. One cannot say as much for his longer works, where certain parts are exaggerated, as in " The Valet de Chambre," " Ward No. 6," " The Steppe," and " The Duel."

The characters of the latter novel are especially weak and bad. There is but one exception, the zoologist von Koren, a man of determination, who believes that the suppression of useless people and degenerates would be a meritorious piece of work. This idea is suggested to him by the sight of a functionary called Layevsky, an insignificant and lazy person, who has taken the wife of one of his friends and fled with her to the Caucasus.

" The Valet de Chambre " is an equally unsatisfactory story. The principal character is a young man who is supposed to be a revolutionist. He enters the service of a Petersburg dandy in hopes of meeting there a minister whom he wants to kill. The employer of the pseudo-lackey, who is not aware of any of his projects, is a masterful presentation of a type which we know as the sybaritical citizen; the character of the valet is so fantastical that the account of his adventures belongs absolutely to the " genre " of the newspaper novel.[3]

" Ward No. 6 " is one of the most powerful, if not the most powerful story that Tchekoff has written. It is an analysis of moral degeneration, leading progressively to insanity, in a doctor who is seized by the pervasive banality of the village in which he practises. Tchekoff, like many other Russian writers, has shown himself a master in the study of certain psychological anomalies. Certain conversations between the doctor, who himself is going mad, and a patient who has long since lost his reason, interesting as they are from a philosophical standpoint, leave the world of reality and run free according to the imagination of the author, who takes advantage of this to formulate some of his favorite theories.

Tchekoff has also tried himself out on the drama, and he has there established himself in a peculiar manner. His plays, like his other literary productions, belong to two distinct periods.

There are some amusing little trifles that do not amount to much. Among these are: "The Bear," "The Asking in Marriage," and others. Then come the more serious plays, where one feels for a moment the influence of Ibsen. We find here again the same heroes, each of whom talks about his own particular case, and acts only in starts. These are specimens of "failures" belonging to the most tiresome provincial society.

In "Ivanov," the author studies the mentality of a "failure." Dominated by a sickly self-love, he has known nothing but losses. He continually complains of his real and his imaginary sufferings. After squandering all his fortune, he marries a young girl, whom he wants to have act as his nurse. This empty life ends in suicide.

In "Uncle Vanya," we have Vanya, a man full of goodness, modesty, and self-abnegation contrasted with the celebrated professor Serebriakof, an egoist, unfeeling, scornful, and ungrateful. The latter, who has recently remarried, comes back to the estate which Uncle Vanya, the brother of his first wife, has managed for him. For several years Vanya has been working incessantly; he has saved in every possible way so that he can send as much money as possible to his brother-in-law, this professor, fondled and pampered by the whole family, who see in him their glorification. But Serebriakof soon gets tired of the country; besides, he thinks that the doctor — a friend of the family who is taking care of him — does not understand his sickness, and he begins to mistrust him. He wants to go away, to travel, in order to recover his health, and, in order to make money, he proposes to sell the estate, which legally belongs to Sonya, the daughter of his first wife.

Up to this time Uncle Vanya and the other members of the family as well, had sacrificed themselves entirely to this celebrated man. But at this proposition Vanya realizes that their idol is nothing but an abominable egoist, and he begins to despise his brother-in-law. What is more, he secretly loves the young and beautiful wife of the professor, while she suffers from the everlasting complaints and caprices of her husband. However, a general reconciliation takes place. The professor and his wife leave for the city, and all goes on as before; Uncle Vanya and the family will sacrifice themselves for the glory of Serebriakof, to whom all the revenues of the estate are sent.

The " Three Sisters," that is to say the sisters of Prozorov, live with their brother in a vulgar, tiresome town, — a town lacking in men of superior minds, a town where one person is like the next.

The great desire of the three sisters is to go to Moscow, but their apathy keeps them in the country, and they continue to vegetate while philosophizing about everything that they see. However, at the arrival of a regiment, they become animated, and have sentimental intrigues with the officers till the very day of their departure.

" They are going to leave; we shall be alone; the monotonous life is going to begin again," cries one of the sisters.

" We must work; work alone consoles," says the second.

And the youngest exclaims, embracing her two sisters, while the military band plays the farewell march:

" Ah, my dear sisters, your life is not yet completed. We are going to live. The music is so gay! Just a little bit more, and I feel that we shall know why we live, why we suffer. . . ."

This certainly is the dominant note of Tchekoff's philosophy: the impotency of living mitigated by a vague hope of progress.

The last, and perhaps the most important play of Tchekoff, is " The Cherry Garden." [4] Human beings, locked up in themselves, morally bounded, impotent and isolated, wander about in the old seignioral estate of the Cherry

Garden. The house is several centuries old. In
former times a happy life was led there; feasts
were given, and generals and princes were the
hosts. The Cherry Garden gave tone to the
neighborhood, but many years have passed!
. . . Now other houses have taken its place:
the estate is mortgaged, the interest is not paid,
and the only guests now are the postman or a
railway official who lives close by. The occu-
pants of the house do not think of doing anything about this state of things. For them the
past is gone. All that is left is a dislike for
work, carelessness, improvidence, and ignorance
of the necessities of the present. Like all that
dies, they evoke a certain pity, a certain fatality hangs over them. The inhabitants of the
Cherry Garden set forth their ideas about one
another; but in reality none of them see anything but themselves, in their small and very
limited moral world, and they analyze with difficulty the embryos of thought that are left to
them. Thus, they cannot grasp in full the evil
that is falling on the old home, and they remain
impassive when some one proposes to alleviate
this evil by energetic means. People speak to
them of the downfall to which they are doomed;
a means of safety is proposed, but they turn a
deaf ear and continue in their narrow and fruit-
less dream. Finally, when the estate is sold,
they look upon this event as a fatal and unex-

pected blow. They say good-bye to the cradle of their family, weeping silently, and depart.

They are now thrown out into the world. The old existence has gone, as well as the seignioral estate. The Cherry Garden is to be torn down; the blinds are all lowered, and in the half-darkened rooms, the old servant, who is nearly a century old, wanders about among the disordered furniture.

Tchekoff is a true product of Russian literature, an autochthon plant, nourished by his natal sap. His humor is completely Russian; we hear Tolstoyan notes in his democracy; the " failures " of his stories are distantly related to the " superficial characters " of Turgenev; finally, the theory of the redemption of the past by suffering which he puts in the heart of the hero of the " Cherry Garden " makes us think of Dostoyevsky. The qualities which call to mind all these great names in Russian literature are found in the works of Tchekoff along with characteristics which show a very original talent. If one wishes to look for foreign influence, one can relate Tchekoff to de Maupassant and Ibsen, of whom he reminds one in snatches, although still in a very vague way. And that is indeed fortunate, for, in general, Scandinavian symbolism hardly goes hand in hand with the Russian spirit, which likes to

make *direct* answers to " cursed questions," and
whose ideal, elaborated since 1840 in the realm
of strict realism, is so definite that it does not
necessitate going back to the circumlocutions
of metaphors and allegories.

While Tchekoff lived his literary aspect was
enigmatical. Some judged him to be indifferent, because they did not find in his writings
that revolutionary spirit which is felt in almost
all modern writers. Others thought of him as
a pessimist who saw nothing good in Russian
life, because he described principally resigned
suffering or useless striving for a better life.
Since the death of Tchekoff, which made it
necessary for the critics to study his works as
a whole, and especially since the publication of
his correspondence, his character has come to
the fore, as it really is: he is a writer, who, by
the very nature of his talent, was irresistibly
forced to study the inner life of man impar-
tially, and who, consequently, remains the
enemy of all religious or philosophical dogmas
which may hinder the task of the observer.

The division of men into good and bad, according to the point of view of this or that
doctrine, angered him:

" I fear," he says in one of his letters,
" those who look for hidden meanings between
the lines, and those who look upon me as a
liberator or as a guardian. I am neither a

liberal nor a conservative, neither a monk nor an indifferent person. I despise lies and violence everywhere and under any form. . . . I only want to be an artist, and that's all."

One realized that this unfettered artist, with his hatred of lies and violence, although he belonged to no political party, could be nothing but a liberal in the noblest and greatest sense of the word. One also realized that he was not the pessimist that he was once believed to be, but a writer who suffered for his ideal and who awakened by his works a desire to emerge from the twilight of life that he depicted.

To some he even appeared as an enchanted admirer of the future progress of humanity. Did he not often say, while admiring his own little garden: " Do you know that in three or four hundred years the entire earth will be a flourishing garden? How wonderful it will be to live then! " And did he not pronounce these proud words: " Man must be conscious of being superior to the lions, tigers, stars, in short, to all nature. We are already superior and great people, and, when we come to know all the strength of human genius, we shall be comparable to the gods."

These great hopes did not prevent him from painting with a vigorous brush the nothingness of mankind, not only at a certain given moment and under certain circumstances, but always and everywhere. Is this a paradox? No. If he did not doubt progress, he would be most pessimistic, if I may so express myself. He would suffer from that earthly pessimism, in face of which reason is weak; the pessimism which manifests itself by a hopeless sadness in face of the stupidity of life and the idea of death.

" I, my friend, am afraid of life, and do not understand it," says one of Tchekoff's heroes. " When, lying on the grass, I examine a lady-bird, it seems to me that its life is nothing but a texture of horrors, and I see myself in it. . . . Everything frightens me because I understand neither the motive nor the end of things. I understand neither persons nor things. If you understand I congratulate you.

" When one looks at the blue sky for a long time, one's thoughts and one's soul unite mysteriously in a feeling of solitude. . . . For a moment one feels the loneliness of the dead, and the enigma of hopeless and terrible life."

This universal hopelessness; this sadness, provoked by the platitudes of existence compared with the unrelenting lessons of death, of which Tchekoff speaks with such a nervous terror, can be found in almost all the works of the best known Russian writers. We find it in Byronian Lermontov, who sees nothing in life but " une plaisanterie; " in Dostoyevsky, who

has written so many striking pages of realism
on the bitterness of a life without religious
faith; and in the realist Turgenev, we find the
same kind of thing. Turgenev even reaches a
stage of hopeless nihilism, and one of his heroes,
Bazarov, — in " Fathers and Sons," — reflect-
ing one day on the lot of the peasant, con-
sidering it better than his, says sadly, " He, at
least, will have his little hut, while all I can hope
for is a bed of thorns." Finally, all the tortu-
ous quests of the ideal toward which Tolstoy
strove, were suggested to him, as he himself
says, by his insatiable desire to find " the meaning of life, destroyed by death."

It is sometimes maintained that this state of
intellectual sadness is innate in the Russians;
that their sanguinary and melancholy temperaments are a mixture of Don Quixote and Ham-
let. Foreign critics have often traced this
despair to the so-called mysticism peculiar to
the Slavonic race.

What is there mystical in them? The consciousness of the nothingness, of the emptiness
of human life, can be found deep down in the
souls of nearly all mankind. It shows itself,
among most people, only on rare tragic occa-
sions, when general or particular catastrophes
take place; at other times it is smothered by
the immediate cares of life, by passions that
grip us, and, finally, by religion. But none of

these influences had any effect on Tchekoff.
He was too noble to be completely absorbed by
the mean details of life; his organism was too
delicate to become the prey of an overwhelming
passion; and his character too positive to give
itself over to religious dogmas. " I lost my
childhood faith a long time ago," he once
wrote, " and I regard all intelligent belief with
perplexity. . . . In reality, the ' intellectuals '
only play at religion, chiefly because they have
nothing else to do." Tchekoff, in his sober
manner, has seen and recognized the two great
aspects of life: first, the world of social and
historical progress with its promise of future
comforts; secondly, an aspect that is closely
related to the above, the obscure world of the
unknown man who feels the cold breath of
death upon him. He was an absolute positivist;
his positivism did not make him self-assertive
nor peremptory; on the contrary, it oppressed
him.

But why should this sad state of mind, which
has been expressed by great men in all literatures, be so exceptionally prominent among the
Russians, and particularly among the modern
ones? The reason is, without a doubt, because
the political and social organization of Russia
has always been a prison for literature. Oppression had reached its height during Tchekoff's life. This period was the moment of suf-

focation before the storm. If Tchekoff were alive to-day, now that the tempest has burst forth, his sadness would be lessened, or it would at least have before it the screen which, according to Pascal, people wear before their eyes that they may not see the abyss, on the edge of which they pass their lives. Up to the present time, the Russians have lacked these screens.

III

VLADIMIR KOROLENKO

" A LONG time ago, on a dark autumn evening, I was being rowed down a rather uninteresting Siberian stream. Suddenly, at a bend in the river, I saw a bright fire burning ahead of us at the foot of some black mountains. It did not seem far away.

" ' Thank Heaven,' I cried with joy, ' we have nearly reached our stopping-place! '

" The boatsman turned, looked at the fire over his shoulder, and again grasped the oars with an apathetic gesture:

" ' That is still a long way off,' he murmured.

" I did not believe him, for the fire seemed to stand out very clear against the infinite shadows. However, he was right; we were still far away.

" Just so those fires, the conquerors of darkness, deceive us into thinking that they are near, while they only cast their distant, illusive rays into the night. . . ."

It is with this sober description in " Little Fires " that one of the last volumes of Korolenko's " Sketches and Stories " opens. This simple picture makes a warm and clear impression on one's very soul. It is itself a precious and welcome light.

At times when life is sombre, and when shadows fill the heart, when, under the blows of despair and anguish, courage finally fails, the mere existence of some brave spirit suffices to give a new birth to hope and to rekindle the flame so that the distance is again lighted up, and we again put our shoulders to the wheel.

Thus for more than thirty years in Russian literature Korolenko has played the part of one of these clear, alluring lights. He has not written a single book in which we do not find a fire that warms us with its caresses even from afar, not one in which we do not feel the vibration of a loving heart, which dreams of giving light and joy to all unfortunates, and is confident that if they have not yet had their equal share, they will surely have it some day.

Korolenko was born in 1853 in Zhitomir, in Little Russia. On his father's side he is descended from an old Cossack family, and by his mother he is related to Polish nobility. This double origin, so to speak, is shown very clearly in his works, which are filled with the melancholy and dreamy poetry of the Little Russians, and also with the perennial hope so common among the Poles.

His father was a judge and enjoyed a repu-

tation for strict integrity. It was, in fact,
often hard for him to ward off those who
wanted to thank him for his services. One day
he had to accept a gift. A merchant, whose
case he had won, sent him a cart filled with
various objects, among which was a beautiful
large doll. The little daughter of the judge
saw it, and at once took possession of it. The
judge, when he found out what had happened,
ordered the gifts to be returned immediately;
but, because of the grief of the little girl, they
had to give up all thoughts of returning the
doll.

The judge, who was a man of firm principles,
maintained a severe discipline in his family.
He made a special study of medicine and
hygiene, and put his knowledge into practice
by treating the sick of the neighborhood. His
children, although always well dressed, had to
go around barefoot. Their father was convinced that this was the best way to toughen
them. Besides, they were compelled, every
morning, summer and winter, to take a cold
plunge bath. The children did not like this
way of doing things. Early in the morning
they used to run to the stable in their shirts,
and there, cowering in a corner, trembling with
cold, they would wait for their father to leave
the house.

Korolenko remembers well this Spartan-like

education, which inured him to the severity of
the seasons. Without this training he certainly
would have perished in savage and freezing
Siberia, where he lived in exile for several years.

At the death of the father, the family with
its six children was left without resources. The
mother, a very good and kind woman, opened
a boys' boarding-school, and Vladimir, then
fifteen years of age, helped her as well as he
could, and also earned money by giving lessons
outside.

In 1870, after having finished his studies in
his native town, Korolenko entered the Tech-
nological Institute at St. Petersburg, where he
spent two years in extreme poverty. He had
to earn his living as well as he could, by giving
lessons or doing copying. His mother could
not help him at all, as she herself had to struggle against adversity. The following will show
how sparingly he had to live in his youth:
during his two years, he had a real substantial
meal only about once in two months, and then
in a restaurant run on philanthropic principles,
where he paid only 30 copecks (about 30 cents).
His regular meals consisted of bread, tea,
sausage and potatoes. But this was an epoch
in which living was cheap: the wave of democracy was spreading, and the " intellectuals "
were trying to get into closer touch with the
people. The movement was so powerful that

many of the younger generation who could have
done other things took up this work; others,
on principle, married humble peasants. In
1872 Korolenko left for Moscow, and there
entered the Academy of Agriculture. He was
expelled after two years and sent to Kronstadt
for having taken part in student manifestations.
Several years later, we find him again in St.
Petersburg without a permanent position; he
was employed as a reader in a publishing house,
and was also attempting to do some writing.
His first efforts took the form of a series of
sketches, published under the title, " Episodes
in the Life of a Seeker." He was at this time
accused of being too much inspired by the
scenes of sadness and injustice of which he had
been a witness. In 1879 he was imprisoned and
then deported to Viatka. He remained there
a year. Thence he was sent to the miserable
town of Kama, and a few months later to
Tomsk, where he learned that they wanted to
exile him to Siberia. In a letter, published by
a newspaper, he eloquently protested against
the persecutions of which he was the unhappy
victim. His protestation was answered by his
transfer to the frozen region of the province
of Yakutsk in Eastern Siberia! He passed
three years in the midst of the " taiga," the
immense virgin forest which covers this country, in a village of nomads whose miserable huts,

very low and smoky, were scattered along the shores of the Aldane. Here he wrote several stories, and the " Dream of Makar," which was published two years later, and greatly praised by the critics for its originality and its setting. The dreary country around Yakutsk and the life that is lived there made such a profound impression on the young man that even to-day he speaks of that time with real emotion.

" My hut was at the extreme end of the town. During the short day one could see the small plain, the mountains which surrounded it, and the fires in the other huts, in which lived people who were either descended from Russian colonists or deported Tartars. But in the morning and evening a cold grey mist covered everything so thickly that one could not see a foot ahead.

" My little hut was like a lost island in a boundless ocean. Not a sound about me. . . . The minutes, the hours passed, and insensibly the fatal moment approached when the ' cursed land ' pierced me with the hostility of its freezing cold and its terrible shadows, when the high mountains covered with black forests rose menacingly before me, the endless steppes, all lying between me and my country and all that was dear to me. . . . Then came the terrible sadness . . . which, in the depths of your heart, suddenly lifts up its sinister head, and in the terrible silence among the shadows murmurs these words: ' This is the end of you . . . the very end . . . you will remain in this tomb till you die. . . .'

" A low and caressing whine brought me out of my heavy stupor: it was my friend, Cerberus, my intelligent and faithful dog, who had been placed as a sentinel near the door. Chilled through and through, he was asking me what was the matter and why, in such terribly cold weather, I did not have a fire.

" Whenever I felt that I was going to be beaten in my struggle with silence and the shadows, I turned to this wholesome expedient, — a large fire."

In 1885, Korolenko, having returned from Siberia, went to Nizhny-Novgorod, and in a relatively short space of time wrote a series of stories which, two years later, were collected in book form. Afterward, he became the editor of the celebrated St. Petersburg review, the " Russkoe Bogatsvo," — a position which he still holds.

In all of Korolenko's works we distinctly feel the living breath that inspires the artist, and the ardor of a fervent ideal. His god is man; his ideal, humanity; his " leitmotiv," the poetry of human suffering. This intimate con-

nection with all that is human is to be found
in his psychological analysis as well as in his
descriptions of natural phenomena. Both God
and nature are in turn spiritualized and human-
ized. Korolenko looks at life from a human
standpoint; the world which he describes is
made up wholly of men and exists for them
only. He has a very clear philosophy, and a
conscience aware of the duties it has to per-
form. If he has not opened up hitherto unknown paths, nor made new roads, he has himself nevertheless passed through terrible experiences; he has been a prey to profound sorrows and doubts, and in spite of all, he has
kept his love for the people intact, and deeply
pities their ignorance and abasement. His work
constantly recalls to our minds the theory that
the cultivated classes are in debt to the people
for the education which they have received at
the people's expense. This is the great moral
principle which governs the conscience of the
Russian " intellectuals." It is in this sense then,
that Korolenko may be said to continue the
literature of 1870, and to be the successor of
Zlatovratsky and Uspensky. But he has re-
incarnated this past in new forms, which naturally result from the activity of his far-sighted,
powerful intelligence. We do not find in his
work either the nervousness, often sickly, which
pervades the works of Uspensky, or the opti-

mism of Zlatovratsky, which often excessively idealizes the life of the Russian peasant, who is the principal hero of all his works. Korolenko, because he puts a high value on human personality, perfectly appreciates the terrible struggle that man has to make in order to secure his rights. A desire for justice on the one hand, and a defence of man's dignity on the other, form the very essence of the talent of this author, and it is with these feelings that he observes the people on whom injustice weighs most heavily and who have merely remnants of human dignity left in their make-up, — for in general, these people are not those whom fate has overcome. Most of them lead a hard and gloomy life beset with misfortunes. Many of them are vagabonds, escaped convicts, drunkards, murderers, who are bowed down with misery, and have no wish except to escape the mortal dangers of the Siberian forests and marshes. On opening any of Korolenko's books we find ourselves, to use his own words, in " bad company." He does not flatter his heroes, he does not make gentlemen of them; they are not even men, but rather human rubbish.

" Because I knew a lot about the world," he writes, " I knew that there were people who had lost every vestige of humanity. I knew that they were corroded with vice and sunk deep in debauchery, in which they lived contented. But

when the recollection of these beings surged
through my mind, enveloped in the mists of the
past, I saw nothing but a terrible tragedy, and
felt only an inexpressible sorrow. . . ."

This author does not give any judgment on
life; he does not condemn it and does not nourish a preconceived spite against it, but his sad
heart overflows with pity, and, if he approaches
this life, it is with the balm of love, in order to
try to dress its terrible wounds.

For Korolenko, the sufferings of existence
atone for its injustice; he does not perceive
the iniquities that surround him except through
the prism of sorrow.

From the very beginning of his literary career, in his first book, "Episodes in the Life
of a Seeker," Korolenko shows himself to be a
seeker after truth. With him, the understanding of life, so ardently sought after, is never
summed up in a single solution. He dreams of
it constantly; at times, he seems to have found
it, but he loses track of it again and starts all
over.

This groping about resulted in a moral crisis
in which he looked forward to death with joy.
Beset with the thought of suicide, he often
prowled around railroad platforms and looked
at the car-wheels.

" I went there and came back again," he

writes, " depressed by my realization of the stupidity of life. The snow was falling all around me, and shaping itself into a frozen carpet, the telegraph poles shivered as if they were cold through and through, and on the other side of the road, on a slope, shone the sad little light of the watchman's tower. There, in the darkness, lived a whole family. Through the shadows the little red fire seemed to be as desolate as the family. The children were scrofulous and suffered; the mother was thin and sickly. To procreate and to bury! Such was the life of the father, probably the most unfortunate of all, because the household depended wholly upon him, and he saw no gleam of hope anywhere. He bore this condition of things, because, in his simplicity, he believed in a superior will, and thought that his misery was inevitable. The resignation of this man, the terrible bareness of his obscure existence, oppressed me. If I could bear the sight of it, it was only because I hoped; I thought that we should soon find the road which makes life happier, more agreeable to every one. How, where, in what manner? What a mystery! But the future beauty of life was in the search for it."

The observations that Korolenko was able to make were many and diverse. By going all

over Russia he gathered inexhaustible riches,
in the form of anecdotes and actual experiences.
This can be easily realized when we consider the
sumptuous variety of his descriptions. Where
do we not go, and whom do we not meet in his
books? First, we are in a peaceful little town
of the southwest, then in the thick woods of
Poliyessye, in the snow-covered and frozen
Siberian forests, or in the valleys of Sakhaline,
inhabited by half-breed Russians and escaped
convicts, not to mention the innumerable
sectarians who fill the Siberian prisons. And
Korolenko never repeats. Not even a detail
occurs more than once. Each of his works is
a little world in itself. The author, moreover,
unlike other writers, is never satisfied with pale
sketches; each character is shown in full relief,
each picture is absolutely finished. This whole-
ness, this finish which does not hurt the harmony of the proportions, is a precious quality,
very rare in our time.

The " Sketches of a Siberian Tourist," published in 1896, in which bandits of various odd
types tell thrilling tales of nocturnal attacks
and other adventures, is a kind of artistic novel.
The postillion is the most original character in
the book. Huge of stature, audacious and
clever, he exercises a mysterious influence over
the brigands, whom he inspires with a super-

stitious terror. Most of them, thinking him
invulnerable, do not dare attack the travelers
whom he is driving.

That same year another work of Korolenko's
appeared, called: " In Bad Company," — a
sort of autobiography which added to his renown. The story, poetically simple, is laid in a
provincial town. The hero is a little, seven-
year-old boy called Volodya. He is the son of
the local judge. The mother has been dead for
a long time, and the father, in his sorrow, more
or less loses track of his children, who roam
about unwatched.

The little town has its historic legends; it
boasts of the ruins of a castle, which in times
gone by was inhabited by rich Polish counts,
whose descendants, having become poor, have
long since left their manorial home. The castle
has served as a refuge for a nomadic population. Expelled by the count's agent, this little
band has taken up its abode in a dilapidated
chapel in the crypts of a cemetery.

The chief of this barefoot brigade is called
Tibertius Droba. He has two children:
Vanek, a large, dark-haired lad, whom one sees
wandering about the village with a sullen look
on his face, and Maroussya, a small and thin
child, who is gradually fading away in the
darkness of her cellar-like home.

While strolling about one day, Volodya, im-

pelled by his childish curiosity, decides, with
two of his friends, to explore the chapel. He
meets there Tibertius' children and they strike
up a friendship. The description of the ruins
and of the superstitious fear of the children
gives an opportunity for some exquisite pages.
If the little vagabonds are hungry, poor Volodya, who himself is without love or caresses,
suffers still more, but every time that he brings
the children some apples or cakes he feels that
he is less unhappy, because these offerings are
accepted with such an outpouring of gratitude.
Gradually, the little lad gets to know all the
inhabitants, and becomes especially intimate
with Maroussya, whose eyes have an expression
of precocious desolation.

" Her smile," says Korolenko, " reminded me
of my mother during the last few months of her
life; so much so, that I almost used to weep
when I watched this little girl."

One day, Volodya brings her some apples,
flowers, and a doll that his little sister has
given him.

" Why is she always so sad? " he asks Maroussya's brother.

" It is on account of the grey stone," he
replies.

" Yes, the grey stone," repeated Maroussya,
like a feeble echo.

" What grey stone? "

" The grey stone that has sucked the life out of her," explained Vanek, gazing at the sky. " Tibertius says so, and Tibertius knows everything."

" I was very much puzzled, but the force with which Tibertius' omniscience was affirmed impressed me. I looked at the little girl, who was still playing with the flowers, but almost without moving. There were dark rings under her eyes and her face was pale. I did not exactly understand the meaning of Tibertius' words, but I felt dimly that they veiled some terrible reality. The grey stone was, in fact, sucking out the life of this frail child. But how could grey stones do it? How could this hard and formless thing worm itself into Maroussya's very soul, and make the ruddy glow disappear from her cheeks and the brilliancy from her eyes? These mysteries puzzled me more than the phantoms of the castle."

Volodya's father is not aware that he is spending part of his days in the cemetery, and knows nothing of his son's new friends. But one day the secret is discovered, and a family storm follows. The judge demands a full confession. Volodya heroically remains silent. Finally, Tibertius himself pleads the child's cause so eloquently that Volodya is not scolded and the father allows him to go and say goodbye to his little friend, who has meanwhile died

of privation. The day after the little girl's
funeral the whole band disappears without
leaving a trace behind them. "Later on," says
Korolenko, "when we were about to leave our
home, it was on the grave of our poor little
friend that my sister and I, both of us full of
life, faith, and hope, interchanged our vows of
universal compassion. . . ."

Another short story, called "The Murmuring Forest," which was published in the same
year, made as much of a success as "Bad Company."

But it is in "The Blind Musician" that
Korolenko attains perfection. This masterly
psychological study does not present a very
complicated plot. From the very start the
reader is captivated by a powerful poetic quality, free from all artifice, fresh, spontaneous,
and breathing forth such moral purity, such
tender pity, that one literally feels regenerated.
Here is a brief outline of this exquisite story.
One very dark night, a child of rich parents is
born in the southwest of Russia. Peter — the
child — is blind. His whole life is to be but a
groping in the shadows toward the light. The
mother adores the poor child and suffers more
than he. But she has not enough moral
strength to bring him up, and give him the
necessary comfort and energy. His father, a

countryman, thinks only of his business. Happily, there is on the mother's side an uncle called Maxim, one of the famous " thousand " of Garibaldi, who has a noble and generous disposition. It is he who brings up the child, with a tenderness just touched by severity. Peter's young mind is constantly enriched with new pictures. Thanks to the extreme acuteness of his hearing, he catches the very slightest sounds of nature. When barely five years of age the boy shows his love for music; he spends hours, motionless, listening to the playing of one of the servants who has made for himself a kind of flute. Soon Peter begins to study music, and especially the violin. His rapid progress astonishes his teachers. However, in spite of his love for music and the comfort that it gives him, the blind boy suffers from his infirmity. To distract his mind from his own suffering, his uncle takes him one day to a place where there are some blind beggars. Peter listens to their plaintive melody: " Alms, alms for a poor blind man . . . for the love of Christ "; and as if he had heard the voice of some phantom, the child returns home, frightened, confused. From that day, he is transformed. Until then, he had thought only of himself, he had become grey with his own sorrow. Afterward, he suffers for others; his personal sorrow diminishes, and his life becomes an expression of the sorrows of his fellows in misery, an ardent and passionate prayer for others who also are deprived of sight.

For several years he has been friends with a young girl of his neighborhood. They marry, and Evelyn, his wife, brings some happiness to the poor blind man. But soon there comes a time of indescribable anguish. Evelyn gives birth to a boy, and Peter is tortured by a presentiment of impending evil. Will the son be blind like his father? The few moments when the doctors are testing the infant's sight pass like so many centuries. Finally the physician says: "The pupil is contracting, the child is not blind." Peter, seated by the window, pale and motionless, rises quickly at these words. In a moment fear has disappeared and hope is transformed into certainty and fills the blind man's heart with joy. "The child is not blind." One might say that these few words of the doctor had burned a path in his brain.

"His whole frame vibrated like a taut cord which had been snapped. A flash went through him, like lightning in a sunless sky, conjuring up in him strange phantasms. Whether they were sounds or sights he could not determine. But if they were sounds they were sounds which he could see. They sparkled like the vault of the sky, shone like the sun, waved like the rustling, whispering grass of the steppes. These were the sensations of a moment. What followed he was unable to recall. But he stubbornly affirmed that in this moment he had *seen.* What had he seen? How had he seen? Had he really seen? This always remained a mystery. People said that it was impossible. He, however, affirmed that in that moment he had seen the earth, his wife, his mother, his son, and Uncle Maxim. . . . He was standing up, and his face was so illumined and so strange that every one around him was silent. . . . Later on, there remained nothing but the remembrance of a sort of joyous satisfaction, and the absolute conviction that, at that moment, he had seen. . . ."

A year later, at Kiev, at a concert for charity, Peter made his début. An enormous crowd gathered to hear the blind musician. From the very first the audience was captivated. Moved to its depths, the crowd became frantic. And Uncle Maxim heard something familiar in the playing of his nephew.

He saw a large, crowded street, and a clear, gay wave of scolding and jesting humanity. Then, gradually, this picture faded into the background. A groaning was heard. It detached itself from the clamor of the crowd and passed through the hall in a sweet but powerful note, which sobbed and moved one's heart. Maxim knew it well, this sad melody: " Alms,

alms for the poor blind man . . . for the love of Christ."

" He understands suffering," murmured the uncle. " He has had his share, and that is why he can change it into music for this happy audience."

" And the head of the old warrior sank on his breast. His work was done. He had made a good man. He had not lived in vain. He had but to look at the crowd to be convinced of that."

Korolenko belongs to the school of Turgenev. In all of his works he remains true to the principles which his master summed up in a letter: " One must penetrate the surroundings, and take life in all its manifestations; decipher the laws by which it is governed; get at the very essence of life, while remaining always within the boundaries of truth; and finally, one must not be contented with a superficial study."

Korolenko lives up to all of these principles. Without tiring, he watches life in all of its phases. He uses a large canvas for his studies of inanimate nature, as well as of individuals in particular and the masses in general. That is why his work gives us such an exact reproduction of life.

Like Turgenev, he describes nature admira-

bly. His descriptions are not irrelevant orna-
ments, but they constitute an organic and integral part of the picture. In both Turgenev
and Korolenko the surrounding country reflects
the feelings and emotions of the heroes, and
takes on a purely lyric character. One might
almost say that these country scenes breathe,
speak a human language, and whisper mysterious legends.

Korolenko has given us several splendid land-
scapes. In some of these nature seems to be
in a serene mood, like a good mother whose
harmonious strength attracts man and shows
him the need of reposing on her bosom. In
others, nature is like a strong, free element
which incites man to lead an independent life.
Thus, in the beautiful prose poem, "The Moment," in which the action passes in Spain, it
is the ocean beating against the prison walls
that arouses Diatz from his torpor and makes
him attempt to escape.

But, in spite of the importance of the background in Korolenko's work, it is really in the
conscience of his characters that the essential
drama takes place. More than anything else,
it is psychology that beguiles the artist; it is
only through psychology that Korolenko depicts men and their mentalities. He studies the
strong and the weak, the simple and the com-

plex; exaltation, triumph, revolt, and downfall all interest him equally.

A simple analysis of his story, "Makar's Dream," will show his psychological genius to greater advantage than could any critical essay.

In the very heart of the dense woods of the "taiga," Makar, a poor little peasant, who has become half savage by association with the Yakutsk people, dreams of a better future.

Makar does not dream, however, when he is normal; he hasn't time to, for he has to chop wood, plough, sow, and grind grain. He only dreams when he is drunk. As soon as he is under the influence of liquor, he weeps and says that he is going to leave everything and go to the "sacred mountain" to gain salvation for his soul. What is the name of this mountain? Where is it? He does not know exactly; he only knows that it is very far away. On Christmas eve, Makar extorts a ruble from two political refugees, and, instead of bringing them some wood for the money, he quickly buys some tobacco and brandy. After drinking and smoking a great deal, Makar goes to sleep and has a dream. He dreams that the frost has got the better of him in the woods, that he has died there, and that the priest Ivan, who has also been dead a long time, takes him to the great Tayon — the god of the woods — to be judged for his former deeds. Even there his

natural knavery does not forsake him; he tries
to fool Tayon. But the latter has everything
that Makar has ever done, both good and bad,
written down, and becoming angry, he says:
" I see that you are a liar, a sluggard, and a
drunkard."

He orders Makar to be transformed into a
post-horse, to be used by the police commis-
sioner. And Makar, this Makar who never in
his lifetime was known to say more than ten
words at a time, suddenly finds that he has the
faculty of speech. He begins by saying that
he does not want to be a horse, not because he
is afraid of work but because this decision is
unfair. If one works geldings, one feeds them
with oats; but people have imposed upon him
and tortured him all his life and have never fed
him, no, not even with oats.

" Who imposed upon you and tortured
you? " asks old Tayon, moved by compassion.

" Everybody! The men who demanded taxes,
the heat and the cold, rain and dryness, the pitiless earth, and the forest."

The beam of the balance wavers; the wooden
dish, filled with sins, rises, while the golden one
sinks.

Makar continues: " You have everything
written down, have you? Well, look and see
whether Makar has ever had any kindness
shown to him. He is here before his judges,

dirty, his hair disordered, and his clothes in rags. He is ashamed. However, he realizes that he was born just like the others, with clear eyes in which both heaven and earth were reflected, and with a heart ready to open and receive all the beauty of the world."

Makar thus passes in review his miserable life. Old Tayon is moved.

" Makar, you are no longer on earth, and you shall receive justice."

Makar begins to weep, and Tayon weeps too. . . . And the young gods and the angels, they also shed tears.

Again the balance moves. But this time it is in the opposite direction.

Makar has received justice from the hands of Tayon.

Korolenko does not try to reconcile us to reality, but to mankind. In all of the catastrophes in his books, in the most sombre descriptions, he comforts us with a consolation, an ideal, a " little fire " that burns in the distance and attracts us. But to get to that fire we have to fight against evil. And it is perhaps in answer to Tolstoy's doctrine of passive resistance that Korolenko wrote that beautiful story called, " The Legend of Florus," the subject of which was probably taken from " The War of the Jews," by Flavius Josephus.

This work takes us back to the time when Judæa was bowed down under Roman rule. The Jews bear their lot without a murmur, and this resignation encourages Florus, the governor of Judæa, to oppress them more.

Soon there are two parties formed: the " pacifics " want to rid themselves of Roman cruelty by humble submission, while the others advise opposing this cruelty to the utmost. The chief of the latter party is Menahem, the son of a famous warrior who has inherited from his father his generous passions and his hatred of oppression. Menahem's words inspire respect even in his enemies. But he does not succeed in making peace among his people. In vain he cries to them, as his father before him had cried: " It is disgraceful to bow down to sovereigns, especially since these sovereigns are men; no human being should bow down to any one excepting God, who created men that they might be free." With great trouble he finally succeeds in rousing a part of the people to rebellion. Then he leaves the city with his followers, resolved to defend his country. Menahem has no illusions as to the outcome; he knows that he will be conquered by the Romans. Nevertheless he is fearless, for his whole being is filled with a single thought, — the idea of justice, which imposes upon men certain obligations which they must not scorn.

During his stay in Siberia Korolenko had a very good chance to observe the deported convicts. Most of them are thieves, forgers, and murderers. The others, urged on by a heroic desire to live their own true lives, have been sent to this " cursed land " because of " political offences."

Korolenko is not resigned to the sadness of life, he is not an enemy to manly calls to active struggle, but he neither wants to, nor can he, break the ties that bind him to the real life of the present. He does not wish either to judge or to renounce this life. Nor does he try, by fighting, to perpetuate a conflict which is in itself eternal. If he struggles, it is rather in discontent than in despair. Not all is evil in his eyes, and reality is not always and entirely sad. His protestations hardly ever take the form of disdain or contempt; he does not rise to summits which are inaccessible to mankind. In fact, his ideal is close to earth; it is the ideal which comes from mankind, from tears and sufferings. If the thoughts and feelings of the author rise sometimes high above the earth, he never forgets the world and its interests. Korolenko loves humanity, and his ideals cannot separate themselves from it. He loves man and he believes that God lives in their souls.

We find these theories in the sketch called

" En Route." The vagabond, Panov, is one
of a party of deported convicts. At one of
the stops, an inspector arrives who remembers
having seen Panov when a young man. The
old man goes over the history of his life, which
has been marked with constant success, with
pleasure. He shows the vagabond his little
son, and with cruel egotism boasts of his happiness. Standing before him, his back bent,
and a sad light in his eyes, Panov listens to the
story. He feels vaguely that he has not lived
and that he lacks personality. There is nothing in store for him except the useless existence
of prison life. The egotistical and debonair
inspector, in his simplicity, does not understand the anguish of the homeless prisoner, and,
by his amicable chatter, subjects him to horrible moral torture. It is too much for Panov.
When the inspector leaves, Panov, gripping the
edge of his hard cot in his convulsive hands,
falls to the ground. He breathes heavily, his
lips move, but he does not speak. " That night
Panov got drunk."

Two very different types appear in the novel
called, " The Postillion of the Emperor." We
have here the idealist Misheka and the sectarian
Ostrovsky, a transported prisoner who is em-
bittered by his hard lot, and by life in general.
If Misheka protests against the complicated
conditions of life to which he cannot entirely

submit, it is rather by instinct than through reason. He is attracted by something invisible, something distant and strange, to the repugnant world which surrounds him. As a postillion of the State he has frequent communications with the distant world which glows vaguely on his mental horizon. Everything displeases him: both the savage country in which he has to live, and the world of stupid, degenerate, and miserable postillions whom he mercilessly criticizes. His random attempts to get away fail. Despairing, he becomes an accomplice in a crime so that he can leave this solitary place and go where his restless soul leads him.

At the side of Misheka we have the tragic figure of Ostrovsky, who is the exasperated victim of the evil all around him.

The author and the travelers, driven by Misheka, have seen the burning of Ostrovsky's house, which the latter burned himself so that no one could profit by it. This action strikes Misheka as wonderful.

" He begins to tell the story of the fire. Several years before, Ostrovsky had been deported for having given up the orthodox faith. His young wife and child followed him. They had been given a plot of land in a broad and deep valley, between two walls of rock. The place seemed fertile. It was not hard to sell

wheat to the miners and Ostrovsky worked dili-
gently and steadily. But the inhabitants had
kept something from him: although the wheat
grew in the valley, it never ripened, because
each year, without fail, in the month of July
it was destroyed by the cold winds from the
northeast."

The first few years Ostrovsky attributed his
failure to chance. He carefully cared for his
crop in the hopes of a better season.

Alas, his wife died of sorrow, and autumn
brought him nothing but straw. Ostrovsky,
without weeping, dug a grave in the frozen
ground and buried his wife. Then he asked
permission to go to the mines, and borrowed
some money for the trip from his neighbors.
The latter gladly loaned it to him, thinking
thus to get rid of him and to get the profit of
his house and goods. But Ostrovsky fooled
them in their naïve simplicity; he heaped up
all of his possessions in his little cottage and
then set fire to it. He no longer thought
of justice; he was nothing but a despairing
man.

The patriarch of the village in which he had
taken refuge tried to recall to him the faith for
which he had been exiled:

" Do you remember," answered Ostrovsky,
" the first visit I paid you to ask for advice?
Ah, so you have forgotten that and you speak

of God. . . . You are nothing but a crafty dog! All of you are dogs! There is nothing here but woods and rocks, and you are all just as insensible as the very rocks that surround you. . . . And your cursed land, and your sky, and your stars. . . ." " He wanted to say something more, but he did not dare blaspheme, and there was silence again in the little cottage. . . ."

This Ostrovsky is among the very best of Korolenko's heroes. The sight of this despairing and lonely man, who wanders about in the Siberian forests with his little daughter, calls louder for justice than all the speeches in the world.

Through the wealth of his talent and knowledge, Korolenko is of tremendous social value in three fields of work, — practical affairs, journalism, and art.

Among the many services which he has rendered to humanity, let us first mention his brilliant defence of the half-savage Votiaks, accused of ritual murder in the famous Malmige case. Although he had just suffered great grief himself — he had lost two children — he traveled to a distant town in order to be at the trial. He took his seat on the bench of the defenders. He used all of his knowledge, and all the love in his heart to defend the unhappy Votiaks, whose acquittal he succeeded in securing.

As a publicist, he has written some very valuable articles. Among them are observations on the famine year (he spent two months in one of the worst districts). In other articles he has analyzed a moral malady peculiar to our state of society: — honor. In the recent Russian duels he studied the perverse notions of honor and the moral changes produced by sickly egotism. He has studied the causes that bring about the complete loss of individuality. Finally, in 1910, he published under the title, " Present Customs (Notes of a Publicist under Sentence of Death) " a series of documents gathered here and there, which constitute an eloquent and passionate plea in favor of the abolitionist thesis.

When the great Tolstoy read the preface of this work, he wrote to Korolenko, " I often sobbed and wept. Millions of copies of this work ought to be distributed; it ought to be read by every one who has a heart. No discourse, no novel or play, can produce the effect that your ' Notes ' do."

But above all, it is as the pure artist that Korolenko merits most attention. It is his talent that has already made him famous, and it is his talent that will make him immortal in Russian literature.

Korolenko is at present one of the most popular writers among the educated classes. They have amply proved this to him, especially in 1903 and 1908, when they celebrated his 50th birthday and the 30th anniversary of his literary activity. On the occasion of these celebrations, delegations from many cities and universities came to St. Petersburg to congratulate and to thank the author who, through so many trials, had never ceased to uphold the cause of truth and goodness, and to claim for each human being the right to work, happiness, and free thought.

IV

VERESSAYEV is well known in France for his "Memoirs of a Physician," a work that has been translated into almost every language. However, his reputation in Russia is not based on this book, which is considered his masterpiece, but rather on his stories and tales. Let us, however, first take a glance at the life of this author, a life so closely connected with the subjects of his works that it forms an indispensable commentary on them.

Veressayev, whose real name is Vikenty Smidovich, was born in 1867, in Tula. His father was a Pole and his mother a Russian. His father, a very pious and strictly moral man, was a well known and well liked physician. In 1877, the boy entered the local school and received his degree there seven years later. In 1884, he left for the University of St. Petersburg, where he enrolled in the department of historical sciences. Four years later, when he was twenty-four and a half, he received his degree of licentiate of letters.[5] Most of his class-mates became school-teachers, but he pre-

ferred to pursue his studies. Medicine tempted
him. He left for Zhouriev (formerly Dorpat,
already famous for its department of medicine)
and entered the university, where, at the end of
six years, he received his doctor's degree.

Two years before, in 1892, a cholera epidemic
had broken out in Russia. Young Smidovich,
then a fourth-year student, asked to be sent
immediately to a province in the East, where the
epidemic was spreading like wildfire. He remained there several months, in fact until the
plague had gone. As a doctor's assistant in an
infirmary organized in one of the mining districts of the government of Ekaterinoslav, he
witnessed a peasant revolt in which several doctors were killed and others cruelly burned by
the exasperated and ignorant mob. Veressayev
has traced these sad events with tremendous
power in his story, " Astray."

His doctor's degree in his pocket, he went
to Tula, where he practised for several months,
but soon the position of house-surgeon was
offered to him in the Botkin Hospital in St.
Petersburg. He remained there seven years,
till 1901, when, by order of the Minister of the
Interior, who has charge of all hospital ap-
pointments, he was forced to retire from office
and was expelled from St. Petersburg and forbidden to reside in either of the two capitals,
Moscow or St. Petersburg. The reason for this

was, that the name Veressayev appeared on the
petition of the " intellectuals " which had been
given to the Minister of the Interior, protesting against the brutal attitude of the police
during a student manifestation in the Kazan
cathedral on March 4, 1901. This petition
brought severe punishment to almost all the
people whose names were signed to it. Veressayev went abroad; he visited Italy, France,
Germany and Switzerland.

Gifted with poetic inspiration, he had begun
writing at an early age. He was not more than
fourteen when he translated some poems of
Koerner and Goethe into Russian verse. Later,
when at college, he wrote some short prose tales,
which were published in various papers. But it
was in 1896, when the " Russkoe Bogatsvo,"
the large St. Petersburg review, had published
his two important stories, " Astray " and " The
Contagion," that renown came to him. It came
so suddenly that it troubled him and was almost
a blow to his modesty, which is one of the sympathetic traits of his personality.

In fact, there came a time when the attention
of the literary world, especially among the
younger generation, became so wrapped up in
his works that Gorky and Tchekoff sank to a
second level. This enthusiasm was caused by
the fact that Veressayev's works answered a
general need. They brought into the world

of literature a series of characters who summed up the rising fermentation of new ideas and seemed to be spokesmen, around whom the Russian revolutionary forces gathered, — forces which, up to this time, had been scattered. An era of struggle for liberty began.

It is rather important, I think, for the proper understanding of this period to say a few words concerning its history.

The struggle of the younger generation against the autocracy began about 1860, at the time of the freeing of the serfs, a period known in Russia as the " epoch of great reforms." These ameliorations, which extended into almost every domain of Russian life, left intact the autocracy, which, under pretence of protecting itself, fought successfully against all activity and thus brought about, among the younger generation, a general movement towards freedom and socialism. But the autocracy found its best help in the ignorance of the people. Urban commerce, little developed at that time, practically interested only the peasants — which means nine-tenths of the population of Russia. It was natural, then, that the peasants should become the principal object of the revolutionary propaganda, and that tremendous efforts should be made on all sides in order to awaken them from their dangerous sleep.

The peasant uprisings in the history of
Russia, especially the two revolts directed by
Stepan Razin in the 17th century, and Puga-
chev in the 18th, proved the fact that the
masses could unite in a general insurrection.
This time, the " intellectuals " joined. As they
advocated a sort of communism, periodic re-
divisions of land according to the growth of
the population, and as they harped on the
tradition that land was a gift of God which
no one had a right to own, we can easily see
that the agricultural proletariat would welcome
with open arms the socialistic ideas.

Although this popular movement did not
affect many people, it was attacked with such
pitiless cruelty, that the revolutionists decided
to have recourse to the red terror in order to
fight the white terror which was cutting down
their ranks. The secret goal of this movement was to replace the autocratic régime with
political institutions emanating from the will
of the people. In order to accomplish its reforms more quickly, this party, which called
itself the " Popular Will," incited several attempts at murder; Russia then witnessed dyna-
mite outrages against imperial trains and
palaces, and finally, the assassination of the
Emperor Alexander II. For a moment the autocratic régime seemed to totter under these
sudden and fierce blows, but it soon recovered.

The white terror proved to be stronger than
the red. Many executions and banishments
helped to crush the partisans of the " Popular
Will; " then, when the movement had been
checked, the authorities began to repress even
the slightest desire for independence on the
part of the press, the universities, or any other
institutions which could do good to the people.
Dejection and disillusion dominated this period
from 1880 to 1900, which has been so faithfully portrayed in the works of Tchekoff.

Nevertheless, in spite of the fact that their
ideals had come to nought, those of the red
terror had not disappeared, and hope remained
in their breasts.

Tchekoff was still living when new symptoms
of fermentation appeared in Russia, and he
could have alluded to this in his later works.
But he did not have a fighting nature, and, in
his solitude, he looked at conditions with
melancholy scepticism. There was need of a
man, a writer — like Gorky several years later
— born right in the midst of this movement,
who would be the very product of it, and for
whom its ideas would be a reason for existence.

Veressayev was this man and writer, and it
is as much by his political opinions as by his
literary talents that he gained such a wide-
spread reputation. If his works are not always irreproachable from a literary standpoint,

they are always accurate in describing exactly
what the author himself has seen and lived
through.

Veressayev, in three great stories, gives us
the three phases of the movement between 1880
and 1900.   These three stories, " Astray,"
" The Contagion " and " At the Turn," are of
such extreme importance, that in the following
pages there will be a detailed analysis of each
of them.

The two protagonists of the story, " Astray,"
are Dr. Chekanhov and his cousin Natasha.   The
former is at the end of his moral life, the latter
is on the threshold, and both of them are
" astray," because the one has not found the
road on which to travel through life, and the
other is just beginning to look for it.   The
entire existence of Chekanhov is dominated by
the idea that it is *his duty to serve the people*,
which was the basis of the activity of the
" narodnikis."   According to him, the " intellectuals," who represent a small and privileged
fraction of the population, are the debtors of
the people and ought to pay their debt by giving the people knowledge and comfort.   This
theory is burned into his very soul; it is the
leading thought that directs all of his actions.
At this epoch, few men showed such absolute
devotion.   From 1880 to 1890, after the cruel

suppression of the movement of the "narod-nikis," there was a stop in this revolutionary activity. Unaware of this pacification, Chekan-hov makes great exertions; as a doctor, he combats disease and saves several people. But how exhaust the source of this evil, this misery, which is increased by a despotic social order? Chekanhov spends his energy in vain; where else shall he apply his strength?

The famine of 1891! Dr. Chekanhov speaks only of his despair: " A terrible malady beats down on one after another of the inhabitants; it is an epidemic of typhoid caused by the privations which left us numb and weak." In 1892 an epidemic of cholera broke out. In spite of the prayers of his parents, the young man rushes off to the most infected district. One day, he penetrates into an infected hovel. The children are sprawling everywhere, the mother is foolish and stupid, and the father, weakened by prison labor, has come down with cholera. The wife forbids the doctor, whom she accuses of poisoning the sick, to approach her husband. Scorning the danger, in order to encourage the sick man, the doctor drinks out of the very cup which the invalid has used. Nothing counts with him as long as he can inspire confidence and save people from death.

" What good is there in love between good and strong people," adds Chekanhov, after hav-

ing noted down this cure in his " Journal,"
" since it results only in miserable abortions?
And why are the people held down to work which
is so rough and unpleasant? What motive sup-
ports them in their painful labor? Is it the
desire to preserve their infected hovels? "

At the end of these reflections could not
Chekanhov, absolutely in despair, have abandoned his task? No, he knew how to keep up
his devotion. Sacrificing his life for others,
Chekanhov begins to love life again. He says
to himself: " Life is good . . . but will it be
for a long time? " We do not catch the answer.

Furious voices are heard, and a savage and
cruel mob calls him a poisoner and hurls itself
upon him, beating and striking him.

Exhausted by the blows and jeered at by
those whom he had considered his brothers in
need and for whom he had put himself in constant peril, he lies stretched out on his bed,
suffering severely; but he nourishes no grudge
against his tormentors; on the contrary, his
apostle-like character is moved with pity at the
thought of these uncultured and ignorant beings so unconscious of the evil that they are
doing. And several days before his death he
writes the following tragic words in his " Journal," almost terrifying in their simplicity:

" They have beaten me! They have beaten

me like a mad dog because I came to help them
and because I used all my knowledge and
strength, in one word, gave all that I had. I
am not thinking now about how much I loved
these people and how badly I feel at the way
they have treated me. I simply did not succeed
in gaining their confidence; I did succeed in
making them believe in me for a while, but soon
a mere trifle was enough to plunge them back
among their dark shadows and to awaken in
them an elemental, brutal instinct. And now I
have to die. I am not afraid of death, but of a
tarnished life full of empty remorse. Why have
I struggled? In the name of what am I going
to die? I am only a poor victim stripped of
the strength of an ideal and cared for by no
one. . . . It had to be so, for we were always
strangers to them, beings belonging to another
world; we scornfully avoid them, without trying to know them, and a terrible abyss separates
us from them."

It is interesting to note how Chekanhov is
regarded by the new generation and especially
by the woman he loves, his cousin Natasha.
She believes in him, she expects a gospel of life
from him; but Chekanhov cannot respond to
her; he adheres to such vague expressions as:
" work," " idea," " duty towards the people."
He says to her: " You want an idea which will
dominate you entirely and which will lead you

to a definite goal; you want me to give you a
standard and say: 'Fight and die for it.' I
have read more than you, I have had more
experience than you, but like you, *I Do Not
Know*, and that is our torture." According
to Chekanhov, all of his generation are in the
same position: it is *Astray*, without a guiding
star, it is perishing without realizing it. . . .
Finally, in order to avoid the pressing questions
of Natasha, who would like to work and sacrifice herself for the poor, he points out to her the
salutary work of the village school-mistress.
A few days later he dies, welcoming death with
joy.

While the people who were ending their existence and those who were beginning it were so
carefully looking for a field of action, the un-
cultivated ground of Russian life was gradually being cleared by the slow evolution of an
economic movement. Between 1895 and 1900,
as a result of the natural development of national commerce, the number of city workingmen grew to vast proportions and they formed
an important class, which, on account of its
situation, was much more qualified than the
peasants to interest itself in the ideas of socialism and liberty. So from the very midst of
the people certain individuals appeared capable of adopting progressive ideas; Marxism

awaited them, the theory which is the basis of
European democratic socialism. This doctrine was nothing new in Russia. But formerly,
the proletariat of the cities had been very little
developed and the Marxian doctrines had been
of theoretical interest only.

"The Contagion" has for its heroine
Natasha, — the Natasha that we have already
met, but how transformed! She has at last
found her bearings. If, in 1892, she was waiting for the right road to be shown to her, in
1896 she was enthusiastically following the new
road opened by the doctrines of Marx.

In Zharoshenko's famous picture, "The
Student," Uspensky notes something new in
this type of femininity. He calls it "the masculine trait"; it is the mark of thought. He
sees there the harmonious fusion of a young
girl and an adolescent boy, with an expression
neither feminine nor masculine, but exceptionally human. And this transforms Zharoshenko's "Student" into a luminous personi-
fication, unknown up to this time, a type which
synthesizes "le type humain."

In the work of Veressayev this student is
Natasha. Reflection has ripened her mind since
her last talk with poor Chekanhov. She has
become a regular "mannish woman," having
seen and thought a great deal. She has traveled; she has lived in St. Petersburg and in the

south of Russia. Full of courage and energy, she claims to be fully satisfied with her lot; she begs her companions to follow the road she has found, and when they refuse she becomes angry with them. In company with her comrade Dayev she vigorously attacks the convictions of the men of Kisselev, who see sufficient safety in the workingmen's associations; she rises up, in the name of Marxism, against the "narodnikis," whom she considers ingenuous idealists; she refuses to endorse the theories of the "intellectuals," who oppose the thought of any great work, since they believe that smaller deeds are more immediately realizable. When one of them, a doctor, Troïtsky, ends his conversation with her with these words: "It is not necessary to wear one's brains out trying to solve difficult problems while there is so much immediate need and so few workers," she puts an end to the discussion. Shrugging her shoulders, in a trembling voice she answers: "How can you live and think as you do? New problems confront us, and you stand before them and do nothing, because you have lost confidence. I can't work any longer with you, because it would mean dedicating myself blindly to 'spiritual death.'"

Veressayev does not show us how she solves the problems of which she speaks. The adepts of this sort of social apostleship usually propagate their ideas among the workingmen, help them, and play a part in conspiracies. Natasha offers herself up. But the censorship has not allowed Veressayev to carry his subject on, and he has limited himself to showing us Natasha in company with her friends and disciples, giving herself up to oratorical tilts, discussing principles, and uttering long discourses full of passion, faith, and juvenile impatience, — discourses which unfortunately are mistaken in their reasoning.

In realizing from the socialist ideal the logical and inevitable consequence of capitalism, which continues according to a law independent of human will, the Marxian doctrine dissipates the doubts and consolidates the faith of those who adopt it. According to this faith, the socialists do not have to create socialism, they only have to coöperate in the historical process which will inevitably make socialism grow. In thus recognizing the supremity of the law of history, socialism, utopian up to this time, becomes scientific and, under its new form, it is no longer subject to the influence of personal opinions, no matter how full of genius they may be. But this " scientific socialism," which, on account of the backwardness of political economy, could be only a step ahead, was taken by the younger generation of Russia as the

" dernier mot " of the science. The result was,
that several narrow and exclusive dogmas were
grafted on this doctrine. Thus, the theory of
" class struggle " transformed itself into the
absolute negation of all community interests
between the diverse social strata. The " mate-
rialistic " — or rather " economic " — point of
view, according to which the products of spiritual activity in the history of humanity lose all
independence, being only the consequences of
economic organization, generated scorn for all
idealism; and the proletariat character of
the socialistic movement impelled society to
divide into two hostile and irreconcilable parts,
one of which is made up of the proletariats, the
other of the elements opposed to socialism. To
this last party the enormous mass of half-
starved peasants joined itself. The peasants,
according to the Marxian doctrine, cannot understand socialism until they have become proletariats themselves, instead of becoming miserable landed proprietors. And this " proletariazation " of about 100,000,000 peasants, the
fervent Marxists consider a fatal and desirable
event in the near future.

These theories, carried to excess, were sure
to excite a reaction. It manifested itself by a
neo-idealistic movement, which found the principal cause of social progress in the tendency
of humanity to attain supreme development and

perfection. Then there were the " narodnikis " who considered the " proletariazation " of the Russian peasant impossible and inopportune. There were also the various groups of Socialists who applauded the criticism that Bernstein made on the Marxian orthodoxy. So several deviations were made from the original theory; there were grave dissensions and interminable and bitter controversies. All this occupies a large part of " At the Turn," one of Veressayev's novels, in which these events are traced with almost stenographic exactitude.

The characters are, Tanya, a fanatic Marxist; her brother, Tokarev, whose soul is a field for spiritual battles; and Varenka, a village school-mistress. There are several eccentric characters around them, such as Serge, a young apostle of a somewhat Nietzschean egoism, Antsov and others. Tanya is none other than Natasha of " Astray," with this great difference, however, that Tanya has found truth already formulated for her, and does not have to grope about for it. Nevertheless, the essential characteristics of the two girls are the same. They both have the same joyous self-denial, the same love of life, the same courage in face of difficulties, and also the same faith in a better future. Tanya has lived during the whole winter with her comrades in a region devastated by the famine, and she has spent there all that she possesses. At Toliminsk, where she arrives after a long walk, she speaks of her meagre living and tells amusing stories without suspecting her wonderful heroism.

But this young girl, full of the joy of life and ready for any sacrifices, is pitiless towards her theoretical adversaries and has absolutely no compassion for them. The passage in " Crime and Punishment," in which Dostoyevsky depicts one of his heroes in the following manner: " He was young, he had abstract ideas, and was, consequently, cruel," perfectly fits Tanya. Veressayev tells the following incident: " One day, when she was at the station, some peasants rushed down from the platform. A railroad guard struck one of the peasants. The peasant put his head down and ran off. . . . Tanya, knitting her brows, said: ' That's good for him! Oh, these peasants!' And her eyes lighted up with scorn and hate. . . ."

Just as Tanya brings Natasha to our mind, so does Varenka make us think of Dr. Chekanhov; the same feeling of duty governs them both. But, while Chekanhov wanted to devote himself to the social problem, without ever succeeding in doing so, because he did not exactly see the principles, Varenka was able to devote herself to her work without mental reservation. However, she refuses to, because she has not enough enthusiasm for this sort of research.

Her understanding, which is deeper and
broader than Tanya's, sees the error, the nar-
rowness of her doctrine; she cannot admit it,
and, fired by a desire to devote herself body and
soul to some useful work, she chooses the laborious profession of a school-mistress in the
village. But this humble and unpleasant career
does not satisfy her. Little by little ennui and
anguish drive her to suicide.

Between Tokarev, Tanya's brother, and
Varenka, the contrast is complete. While still
a student, he had accepted, with all the ardor
of youth, the idea of duty, and he desired to
give himself up to the cause of justice and
truth; but, having encountered many obstacles,
he felt, when he had reached his thirtieth year,
that the sacred fire was going out.

He now dreamed only of his personal happiness, and of poor theories that justified this
egoism. An assured material existence, comfort, a happy domestic life, work without risks,
without sacrifices, but useful enough in appearance to satisfy the conscience, attracted him irresistibly. He then went to work to tear out
his former ideas, which had taken a pretty firm
root. Urged on by his conscience, which protested, he forced himself at times to resurrect
his youthful enthusiasm; he thought a great
deal about morals, about duty, and he read
many books treating this subject; he says: " I

feel that something extremely necessary has left me. My feelings about humanity have disappeared and nothing can replace them. I read a great deal now, and I am directing my thoughts towards ethics. I try to give morality a solid basis and I try to make clearer to myself the various categories of duty. . . . And I blush to pronounce the word, ' Duty.' "

Nevertheless, Tokarev tries, at times, to justify his inclinations towards peaceable bourgeois prosperity to the struggling youth who surround his sister Tanya. These cruel young people, however, answer him only with sarcastic remarks, and caustic arguments, and do not hesitate to express their doubts as to the sincerity of his opinions. To his conscience, they are like a living reproach from the past. Once he also was intolerant towards others as these people are towards him to-day. And that is why he suffers under their condemnation of him. He defends himself weakly, and after one of his oratorical tilts, he falls into such spiritual depression, that he almost thinks of suicide.

These, then, are the three main characters of Veressayev's novel. In the background we have the secondary characters. We have the proud proprietor and his wife, both of them liberals; we have the pedagogue Osmerkov, who does not like talented people because they bother everybody; and then there are the respectable inhabitants of Gniezdelovka, Serge's father and mother, who are entirely absorbed with their household and with cards.

" The Comrades " is a variation on this theme: old school friends, who formerly had been wrapped up in a great ideal, are now living a life of shabby prosperity, and they feel that they have deteriorated, although they do not dare to confess it to each other.

And Veressayev profits by this to generalize on the causes of this fatal fall after the unselfish enthusiasms of youth. He sees them especially in a mysterious force: " The Invisible," already studied by Maeterlinck, Ibsen, Tchekoff, and especially by de Maupassant; and he sees them in the unhappy conditions of Russian history, which created a social and political organization favorable only to those who crawl along and not to those who plan.

Let us now analyze the stories in which Veressayev describes the life of the people.

The story of " The Steppe " is as follows: One beautiful autumn evening two men meet on the steppe. One of them, the forger Nikita, is returning to his native land; he is wounded in the leg and it is hard for him to walk. He is looking for work. The other is a professional beggar.

The beggar, who is never hungry because he has no scruples, offers Nikita something to eat. After resting a short while, the travelers continue on their way. In the first village that they come to, the pilgrim beggar makes a speech to the inhabitants and sells them certain " sacred properties " which he keeps in his bag. After pocketing gifts of money and various other things, the false pilgrim pursues his way, still accompanied by Nikita. On the road once more, he offers to share with his comrade the fruits of his " work," but the latter refuses.

" What a fool! " cries the beggar, and bursts out laughing. But Nikita, indignant, gives him a heavy blow and leaves him for good.

" For a Home " and " In Haste " gave Veressayev an opportunity to note one of the characteristic traits of the ambitious villagers: their strong desire to preserve their homes and to propagate the race.

In the first of these stories, two old people, Athanasius and his wife, want to marry their daughter Dunka, but the " mir," — the assembly of peasants, — egotistical and inflexible towards people who are growing weak, oppose them. " We have not enough land for our own children," is the answer of the " mir." Dunka remains unmarried, and dies at an early age. Her mother soon follows her. Old Athanasius lives alone in his freezing " isba," which is in a state of ruin, while the neighboring isbas, solid and austere, " spitefully watch him die."

In the last story, we have a widower who is the father of five children, and is therefore looking everywhere for a woman with some bodily defect, because he knows that other women will not want to have anything to do with him.

It is the same wish to preserve his home that makes a peasant go to the city to earn his living while he leaves his family in the country to take care of the house.

The peasant is, besides, entirely engrossed with the difficulties of existence. Necessity often urges him to desperate acts. . . . Some, who are almost starving, ingratiate themselves with the raftsmen. They force wages down by asking only 5 copecks (5 cents) a day. . . . If they are contented with this absurd pay, it is because they avoid seeing how their little children are suffering at home. " It's hard living at present; there is not enough space; ground is scarce and there are too many people." " Men haven't room enough," says a sad-looking man with prominent cheek-bones. " But," he goes on, " they tell me that sickness has struck our village, and that the men are losing blood! Is that true? " " Yes, it's true! " " So much the better! That will clean out the

people; it will be easier to live then," he concludes, thoughtfully.   (From " In the Cold
Spell.")

In almost all the work of Veressayev a voice
proclaims that the Russian peasant is near his
end; that he is not useful to any one. The
poverty of the villages is painted in the most
sombre colors. The people are unanimous in
believing that the struggle for life has become
terrible. " On what will you live? " one asks
the other. " The earth does not nourish us.
The holdings are small; in summer, one must
cultivate, and in winter the cottages have to
be closed while we look for work or charity.
What is there to eat? Hay! Let us thank God
that the cattle have enough of that. Oats? We
have to give four hectoliters and two measures
of our oats to the common granary. . . . And
taxes and clothes? coal-oil, matches, tea,
sugar? Tell me, how can one live? "

The unfortunates even go so far as to bless
war and epidemics. " Everything went better
then. Men lived peacefully in the fear of God,
the Lord took care of every one. War, small-
pox, famine came and cleaned out the popu-
lace; those that remained, after having got the
coffins ready, lived easier. God pitied us. Now
there is no more war; He leaves us to our own
poor devices."

Speeches like this abound in the works of

Veressayev. A dull sadness, bordering on despair, breathes forth from the pages. It seems, at times, as if the Russian peasant could never awake from his torpor, because the author represents him as full of infinite egoism, without any spirit of solidarity, sacrificing everything for love of his sorry little house and his morsel of ground, which is insufficient to nourish him. But we must remember that the Marxian point of view, which the author takes, explains in part the horror of such pictures.

According to Veressayev the poor peasants can better their position only by getting rid of their land, in order to become free proletarians. But if the peasant class is unfortunate, it is so, for the most part, because it is the most exploited and the most oppressed. It is not, then, the getting rid of their land that will bring the peasants salvation; on the contrary, they must fight for it against their oppressors. The peasants are beginning to understand the necessity of this struggle, and their late uprisings in several provinces have shown that they lack neither solidarity nor organization.

In the story called, " The End of Andrey Ivanovich," which is about the working class of Russia, we see the transformation of a peasant into a " city man." In his new surroundings, it is true, the wine-shop plays an important rôle, but schools are organized there which inspire a taste for reading, and " thought " gradually awakens.

Andrey has not yet rid himself of his rustic unsociability; however, he is beginning to become civilized, and is receiving city culture. He tries to free himself from his misery, from his degradation. He beats his wife when he is drunk, but, at the same time, he gets angry at a friend when he beats his mistress. . . . According to his own confession he reads many useless things, nevertheless he can become interested in a serious work. If he drinks to excess, it is to " drive away the thoughts " that torment him. He wants to analyze every question and find out what is at the bottom of it. He is the spiritual brother of Natasha, Chekanhov, and Tanya.

The sequel to this story is " The Straight Road." This time we are transported into the world of factory workers, a world lamentable for its misery, despair, and crime. Andrey Ivanovich's wife, Alexandra Mikhailovna, being without resources after the death of her husband, with a little daughter in arms, enters a book-binding establishment, belonging to a man named Semidalov. But the foreman, a vicious and evil-minded man, reigns as despot. It is he who gives out the work. The young

girls who listen to his advances are sure of
being shown partiality; the others are badly
treated. As Alexandra wants to live honestly,
her work in the shop is made very hard. Her
best friend, Tanya, who inadvertently spilled
oil on some paper and could not pay for the
damage, had to give herself to the foreman.
Finally Tanya despairs and ends by drowning
herself. Alexandra is saved, thanks to a " love-
less " marriage with the locksmith, Lestmann.
She accepts this union so that she will not have
to starve and can remain " straight." Thus,
the " straight road " which Alexandra wanted
to follow has forced her finally to sell herself,
to marry a man whom she does not love.

Each page of Veressayev's work exists
merely to throw light on this or that social
question, considered from a well defined point
of view. The secret of his success rests mostly
in the frank, sincere manner in which he has
approached certain problems. At the same
time, all of his work breathes forth a deep and
tender love for those who suffer. In reality,
there is not a single book by Veressayev which
might not be a confession; all that he writes
he has already experienced himself, and his
work vibrates with a delicate and personal emotion. It is only necessary to read, " The Memoirs of a Physician," which is almost an auto-

biography, in order to perceive the moral relationship that exists between Veressayev and the heroes of his stories.

This book is the confession of a physician from the time of his early studies. The young man is astonishd at the number of maladies that exist and by the unbelievable variety of keen suffering that nature inflicts upon the human species, man. Soon he is obliged to make a discovery that stuns him: that medicine is incapable of curing many evils. It only gropes about, trying thousands of remedies before it arrives at a sure result. The scruples and anxiety of the student increase, especially after an autopsy on a woman in the amphitheatre, when the professor announces that the woman has succumbed because the surgeon, who was operating, swooned, and ends by saying: " In such difficult operations the very best surgeons are not safe from accidents of this kind." After this, the professor shook hands with his colleague and every one left. At that time, doubt entered the mind of the young man. And so, within a period of ten years, he passes from extreme optimism to the same degree of pessimism.

We follow him in the hospitals, where he is scandalized by the brutality of the teaching, which makes use of the unwilling bodies of sick people. " Not being able to pay for their treatment in money, they have to pay with their bodies." Finally, the student becomes a doctor himself. Full of faith and knowledge, he starts practice in a small market-town of central Russia. But his work soon cools him down; in the clinic he had studied mostly exceptional cases; now he is disconcerted by simple and every-day sicknesses. His ignorance leads to the following tragic case:

One day, a poor and widowed washerwoman brings him her sick child, whom she does not want to take to the hospital because her two oldest children died there. The child is a weak boy of eight years who has caught scarlet-fever. At first, the inside of the throat begins to swell, and, to prevent an abscess, the doctor orders rubbings with a mercurial ointment. The next day, he finds the boy all aquiver and covered with pimples. " There is no mistake," he says, " the rubbing has spread the infection into the neighboring organs and a general poisoning of the blood has taken place. The little boy is lost. . . . All that day and night I wandered about the streets. I could think of nothing, and I felt crushed by the horror of the thing. Only at times this thought came into my mind: ' I have killed a human being ! ' " The child lived ten days more. The night before his death Veressayev comes to see him. The poor mother is sobbing in a corner of the

miserable room. She pulls herself together,
however, and taking three rubles out of her
pocket, offers them to the trembling doctor,
who refuses them. Then this woman falls down
on her knees and thanks him for having pitied
her son. "I'll leave everything, I'll give up
everything," sobs the doctor. . . . "I have
decided to leave for St. Petersburg to-morrow
in order to study some more even if I die of
hunger!"

Once the resolution was made to pursue his
studies in a more practical manner, he becomes
the house-surgeon of a hospital. But even
there a mass of problems disturb him. He sees
how dangerous the simplest operations are; he
is frightened by the unrestraint of the doctors,
who try new methods on the sick, methods the
effects of which are not known, methods that
result in the patient's being inoculated with
more sickness. Medicine cannot progress without direct experimentation, and experience is
gained at the expense of the more unfortunate.
Nevertheless, Veressayev does not argue
against this way of working; he shows the
facts, and leaves it to the reader to decide. On
the other hand, he does not hide his fear of the
common ignorance of all doctors. Every individual differs from his neighbor. How distinguish their idiosyncrasies? Once the scope
of a sickness is known, what remedy shall be

used? Some say this, others, that. How shall one choose? Veressayev has felt all of this; he has tried to harden himself against the unreasonable ingratitude of some, the scepticism of others; he realizes that patience, resignation, and heroism are needed in order to struggle against and support the mortifications in the career of a doctor. How much easier it would be not to consider medicine as infallible; to study it as an art rather than as a science. But people prefer to believe that doctors know everything. They do not want to see the reality, and this is the reason why sad, and at times tragic conflicts arise between patient and physician.

Finally, what could the most perfect medical science and the cleverest doctor do against the enormous mass of sickness and suffering that are the inevitable result of the social evils, of which poverty is the most conspicuous? How can one tell a man that his trade is running him down and that he does not get enough nourishment? How can one order a man to eat better food, to get more sleep and more pure air? First, and most important, is the necessity of curing the social organism.

It is easy to see why this book made many enemies for its author. There is too much frankness and conscientiousness in these studies not to anger those who have their greatest interest in concealing the truth! The upright man who sees primarily in medicine a means to relieve human suffering, cannot realize without sadness the many abuses hidden under the name of this science.

" In the War," recently published, is the story of Veressayev's campaign in Manchuria. In this work, the author has painted vividly the peregrinations of his moving hospital, and also the terrible sufferings of the Russian army. By the thousands, the starved children of the campaign, the Russian foot-soldiers, stoics and fatalists, sacrificing their lives for a strange and incomprehensible cause, pass before the eyes of the reader. And in the background, detaching themselves from the crowd, in their gold and silver embroidered uniforms, are " the heroes of the war, these vultures of the advance and rear-guard, who enrich themselves at the expense of the unfortunate soldiers." A number of these great chiefs, whose infamy was evident at the end of the war, since they had shown themselves incapable of dealing with the foreign enemy, had distinguished themselves by the ferocity they exhibited in quelling internal troubles. As to the military doctors, the greater number of them went into the campaign only for commercial gain. Among the nurses who accompanied them, aside from those who were real heroines of goodness and devotion, there were many who prostituted themselves shamefully.

Corruption, carelessness, disorder, and cowardice are shown on every page of this story, as well as the terrible suffering endured by the wounded in the hospitals. The wounded were the real martyrs of this frightful campaign.

Veressayev, like all of his heroes and heroines, wants to help the people, and for this reason he gets in touch with the revolutionists who consecrate their work to political and social regeneration, under the various titles, " narodnikis," Marxists, Socialists, idealists and so on. . . . Which of these does he prefer? We do not know. We find the influence of Marx in his ideas, but we cannot affirm that he is an absolute Marxian. It seems as if Veressayev, troubled by the innumerable divergencies of opinion, asks himself secretly: " Will this war lead to the unity of opinion and program, so necessary for victory, or by its quarrels will it only retard the harmony so much sought after? "

It is not discussion that will finally lead to unity, but rather life itself, with all its realities.

It would be most interesting to read a sequel to the three famous novels of Veressayev —

"Astray," "The Contagion," and "At the Turning" — in which he would give us the psychology of his former heroes under present conditions. To-day, the people are not "astray"; the field is big enough for every one to find the place that best suits his ideas, tastes, and temperament. Dr. Chekanhov, if he were living now, instead of being maltreated by the people, would certainly be their well beloved champion, and perhaps represent them in the Duma; the timid Tokarev, in spite of his aversion to the ideas of the revolutionists, could find a place in the liberal party of the Reforming Democrats, or at least among the Octobrists; the unfortunate Varenka would not be worn out by her work as school-mistress, for she would be supported by the peasants. The peasants themselves are not the miserable and resigned creatures of Veressayev's earlier stories. Certainly, liberty is not yet a legal thing in Russia, and the Duma is still an unstable institution, but the end of absolutism is near, for a great event has taken place in the empire of the Tsar, namely, this awakening of the feeling of human dignity, and the spirit of revolt among the lower strata of the Russian people, which in the past, by its unconsciousness, formed the granite pedestal of autocracy. The struggle is terrible, but confidence in final victory redoubles the energy of the strugglers.

A certain Russian was right when he said:
" Formerly, life was formidable, but now it is
both formidable and gay."

In reading the works of Veressayev, Tchekoff, and other painters of modern Russian
society, it is easy to note that not one of
them anticipated this sudden change of scenery
on the Russian political stage, a change which,
however, was being prepared in the souls of the
peasants. But let us not reproach them!
Russia will always remain an enigma.

There is a very old story about the son of
the peasant Ilya Murometz. After remaining
lazily resting in his " isba " for thirty years, he
suddenly arose, and began to walk with such
fury that the earth trembled. How could these
writers conceive the time when this lazy giant
would make up his mind to walk? It is enough
to have the assurance that now, no matter what
happens, since he *has* arisen, he will not lie
down again.

V

MAXIM GORKY is the most original and, after Tolstoy, the most talented of modern Russian writers. He was born in 1868 or 1869 — he does not know exactly when himself — in a dyer's back shop at Nizhny Novgorod. His mother, Barbara Kashirina, was the daughter of the aforementioned dyer; and his father, Maxim Pyeshkov, was an upholsterer. The child was christened Alexis. His real name, then, is Alexis Pyeshkov, and Maxim Gorky [6] is only his pseudonym. When he was four, he lost his father, and three years later, his mother. He was then taken by his grandfather, who had been a soldier under Nicholas I, a hard, authoritative, pitiless old man, before whom all trembled. And it was under his rude tutelage that the child first began to read. When he was nine, he was sent to work for a shoemaker, an evil sort of man who maltreated him.

"One day," Gorky tells us, "I was warming some water for him; the bowl fell, and I burned my hands badly. That evening I ran away,

142

my grandfather having scolded me severely. I then became a painter's apprentice."

He did not remain long in this position. From this time on, his unsatisfied soul was seized with the " wanderlust." First apprenticed to an engraver, and then as a gardener, he finally became a scullion on one of the boats that plies up and down the Volga. Here he felt more at ease.

On board, in the person of the master-cook, named Smoury, he unexpectedly met a teacher. This cook, who had been a soldier, loved to read, and he gave the child all the books that he had in an old trunk. They consisted of the works of Gogol, Dumas' novels, the " Lives of the Saints," a manual of geography, and some popular novels. Surely, a queer collection!

Smoury inspired his scullion, then sixteen years of age, " with an ardent curiosity for the printed word." A " furious " desire to learn seized the young fellow; he went to Kazan, a university city, in the hope of " learning gratuitously all sorts of beautiful things." Cruel deception! They explained to him that " this was not according to the established order." Discouraged, a few months later, he took a position with a baker. He who dreamed of the sun and the open air had to be imprisoned in a filthy and damp cellar. He remained there for two years, earning two dollars a month, board and lodging included; the food, however, was putrid, and his lodging consisted of an attic which he shared with five other men.

" My life in that bakery," he has said, " left a bitter impression. Those two years were the hardest of my whole life." He has thus described his recollections in one of his stories:

" We lived in a wooden box, under a low and heavy ceiling, all covered with cobwebs and permeated with fine soot. Night pressed us between the two walls, spattered with spots of mud and all mouldy. We got up at five in the morning and, stupid and indifferent, began work at six o'clock. We made bread out of the dough which our comrades had prepared while we slept. The whole day, from dawn till ten at night, some of us sat at the table rolling out the dough, and, to avoid becoming torpid, we would constantly rock ourselves to and fro while the others kneaded in the flour. The enormous oven, which resembled a fantastic beast, opened its large jaws, full of dazzling flames, and breathed forth upon us its hot breath, while its two black and enormous cavities watched our unending work. . . ."

" Thus, from one day to the next, in the floury dust, in the mud that our feet brought in from the yard, in the suffocating and terrible heat, we rolled out the dough and made cracknels, moistening them with our sweat; we hated

our work with an implacable hatred; we never
ate what we made, preferring black bread to
these odorous dainties."

At this period of his life, he had occasion
to study at first hand certain places where he
received original information which he later used
in writing "Konovalov" and "The Ex-Men,"
which have thus acquired an autobiographical
value. In fact, he worked a long while with
these "ex-men;" like them, he sawed wood,
and carried heavy burdens. At the same time,
he devoted all his spare time to reading and
thinking about problems, which became more
and more "cursed" and alarming. He had
found an attentive listener and interlocutor in
the person of his comrade, the baker Konovalov.
These two men, while baking their bread, found
time to read. And the walls of the cellar heard
the reading of the works of Gogol, Dostoyevsky, Karamzine, and others. Then they used
to discuss the meaning of life. On holidays,
Gorky and Konavolov had for the moment an
opportunity to come out of the hole — this
word does not exaggerate — in which they
worked, to breathe the fresh air, to live a bit
in nature's bosom, and to see their fellow men.
"On holidays," Gorky tells us, "we went
with Konovalov down to the river, into the
fields; we took a little brandy and bread with

us, and, from morning till evening, we were in
the open air."

They often went to an old, abandoned house
which served as a refuge for a whole tribe of
miserable and wandering people, who loved to
tell of their wandering lives. Gorky and his
companion were always well received on account
of the provisions which they distributed so generously.

" Each story spread out before our eyes like
a piece of lace in which the black threads predominated — they represented the truth — and
where there were threads of light color — they
were the lies. These people loved us in their
way, and were attentive listeners, because I
often read a great deal to them."

Often, these expeditions were not without
their risks. One day, two of the baker's workmen happened to drown in a bog; another time,
they were taken in a police raid and passed the
night in the station house.

It was also at this time that Gorky fre-
quented the company of several students, not
care-free and happy ones, but miserable young
fellows like those whom Turgenev described as
" nourished by physical privations and moral
sufferings."

On leaving the bakery, where his health, very
much weakened by the lack of air and by bad
food, did not permit him to remain any longer,

he joined those vagabonds, those wanderers, whose melancholy companion he had been, and whose painter and poet he was to be. In their company, he traveled through Russia in every sense of the word, now as a longshoreman, now as a wood-chopper. Whenever he had a copeck in his pocket he bought books and newspapers and spent the night reading them. He suffered hunger and cold; he slept in the open air in summer, and, in winter, in some refuge or cellar. The feverish activity of so keen an intellect in an organism so crushed had, as its consequence, one of the attempts at suicide which are so frequent among the younger generation of the Russians.

In 1889, at the age of twenty-one, Gorky shot himself in the chest, but he did not succeed in killing himself. Soon afterwards, he became gate-keeper for the winter at Tzaratzine; but the summer had hardly come before he began his vagabondage again, in the course of which he undertook a thousand little jobs in order to keep himself alive. On the road, he noticed those pariahs whom society does not want or who do not want society. And of these, in his short stories, he has created immortal types.

Life was still very hard for him at this time. He has given us a moving sketch of it in his story entitled: " Once in Autumn." The hero,

who is none other than the author himself,
passes the night under an old, upturned boat,
in the company of a prostitute who is just as
poor and just as abandoned as himself. They
have broken into a booth in order to steal
enough bread to keep them from starving.
Gorky is sad; he wants to weep; but the poor
girl, miserable as she is, consoles him and covers
him with kisses.

" Those were the first kisses any woman ever
gave me, and they were the best, for those that
I received later always cost me a lot and never
gave me any joy. . . . At this time, I was already preparing myself to be an active and
powerful force in society; it seemed to me
at times that I had in part accomplished my
purpose. . . . I dreamed of political resolu-
tions, of social reorganization; I used to read
such deep and impenetrable authors that their
thoughts did not seem to be a part of them —
and now a prostitute warmed me with her body,
and I was in debt to a miserable, shameful creature, banished by a society that did not want
to accord her a place. The wind blew and
groaned, the rain beat down upon the boat, the
waves broke around us, and both of us, closely
entwined, trembled from cold and hunger. And
Natasha consoled me; she spoke to me in a
sweet, caressing voice, as only a woman can.
In listening to her tender and naïve words, I

wept, and those tears washed away from my heart many impurities, much bitterness, sadness and hatred, all of which had accumulated there before this night."

At daybreak, they say good-bye to each other, and never see one another again.

" For more than six months, I looked in all the dives and dens in the hope of seeing that dear little Natasha once more, but it was in vain. . . ."

We find him again at Nizhny Novgorod at the time of the call for military recruits. Gorky was reformed, for, he says, " They do not accept those who are fallen." Meanwhile, he became a kvass merchant and exercised this trade for several months. Finally, he became the secretary of a lawyer, named Lanine. The latter, who had a very good reputation, took a deep interest in the poor boy whom life had treated so ill. He became interested in his intellectual development and, according to Gorky himself, had a great influence on him. At Nizhny Novgorod, as at Kazan, Gorky felt himself attracted by the circle of young people who discussed the " cursed " questions, and he soon was noticed by his comrades. They spoke of him as " a live and energetic soul."

Easy as life was for Gorky in this city, where he remained for a while, the " wanderlust " again seized him. " Not feeling at home among these intelligent people," he traveled. From Nizhny Novgorod, he went, in 1893, to Tzaratzine; then he traveled on foot through the entire province of the Don, the Ukraine, entered into Bessarabia, and from there descended by the coast of the Crimea as far as Kuban.

In October, 1892, Gorky found himself at Tiflis, where he worked in the railroad shops. That same year, he published in a local paper his first story, " Makar Choudra," in which already a remarkable talent was evident.

Leaving Tiflis after a short sojourn there, he came to the banks of the Volga, in his native country, and began to write stories for the local papers. A happy chance made him meet Korolenko, who took a great interest in the " debutante " writer. " In the year 1893-1894," writes Gorky, " I made the acquaintance of Vladimir Korolenko, to whom I owe my introduction into ' great ' literature. He has done a great deal for me in teaching me many things."

The important influence of Korolenko on the literary development of Gorky can best be seen in one of the latter's letters to his biographer, Mr. Gorodetsky. " Write this," he says to his biographer, " write this without changing a single word: It is Korolenko who taught Gorky to write, and if Gorky has profited but little by

the teaching of Korolenko, it is the fault of
Gorky alone. Write: Gorky's first teacher was
the soldier-cook Smoury; his second teacher
was the lawyer Lanine; the third, Alexander
Kalouzhny, an ' ex-man;' the fourth, Korolenko. . . ."

From the day when he met Korolenko,
Gorky's stories appeared mostly in the more
important publications. In 1895, he published
" Chelkashe " in the important Petersburg review, " Russkoe Bogatsvo; " a year later,
other publications equally well known published, " Konovalov," " Malva," and " Anxiety."
These works brought Gorky into the literary
world, where he soon became one of the favorite
writers. The critics, at first sceptical, soon
joined their voices with the enthusiastic clamor
of the people.

Gorky's wandering life has given his works
a peculiar and universally established form.
He is, above all others, the poet of the " barefoot brigade," of the vagabonds who eternally
wander from one end of Russia to the other,
carelessly spending the few pennies that they
have succeeded in earning, and who, like the
birds of the sky, have no cares for the morrow.
But this does not suffice to explain this author's popularity, especially among the younger
generation. The " barefoot brigade " is not

a novelty in Russian literature. We find it in
the works of Reshetnikov, Uspensky, Mamine,
Zhassinsky, and others. It is true that, up to
this time, the vagabonds had been represented
as the dregs of the people, as hopeless drunkards, thieves, and murderers. The writers who
represented them were satisfied in rousing in
their readers pity for the victims of this social
disorder, victims so wounded by fate, that they
have not even a realization of the injustice with
which they are treated. And it is only in the
works of the great dramatist Ostrovsky that we
find any happy vagabonds, with a deep love of
nature and beauty.

Gorky's vagabonds have, like Ostrovsky's,
exalted feelings for natural beauties, but they
possess, besides, a full consciousness of themselves, and they declare open war against
society. Gorky lives the lives of his heroes; he
seems to sink himself into them, and, at the
same time, he idealizes them, and often uses them
as his spokesmen. Far from being crushed by
fate, his vagabonds clothe themselves with a certain pride in their misery; for them, the ideal
existence is the one they lead, because it is free;
with numerous variations, they all exalt the irresistible seduction of vagabondage:

"As for me, just listen! How many things
I've seen in my fifty-eight years," says Makar
Choudra. "In what country have I not been?

That is the only way to live. Walk, walk, and
you see everything. Don't stay long in one
place: what is there out of the ordinary in that?
Just as day and night eternally run after one
another, thus you must run, avoiding daily life,
so that you will not cease to love it. . . ."

"I, brother," — says, in turn, Konovalov, —
"I have decided to go all over the earth, in
every sense of the word. You always see something new. . . . You think of nothing. . . .
The wind blows, and you might say that it
blows the dust out of your soul. You feel free
and easy. . . . You are not troubled by any
one. If you are hungry, you stop, and work
to earn a few pennies; if there is no work to
be had, you ask for some bread and it is given
to you. So you see many countries, and the
most diverse beauties. . . ."

Likewise, in "Tedium," Kouzma Kossiyak
thus clearly expresses himself:

"I would not give up my liberty for any
woman, nor for any fireplace. I was born in a
shed, do you hear, and it is in a shed that I am
going to die; that is my fate. I am going to
wander everywhere until my hair turns grey.
. . . I get bored when I stay in the same place."

In their feeling of hostility to all authority,
and all fixed things, including bourgeois
happiness and economical principles, some of
Gorky's characters resemble some of those supe-

rior heroes of Russian literature, like Pushkin's
Evgeny Onyegin, Lermontov's Pechorine, and,
finally, Turgenev's Rudin, who, in their way,
are vagabonds, filled with the same independent
spirit in their respective social, intellectual, or
political circles.

On the other hand, Gorky's wandering beggars are closely related to those " free men " to
whom M. S. Maximov attributes a historic rôle
which was favorable to the extension of the
Russian empire. " Russia," he says, in his book,
" Siberia and the Prison," " lived by vagabondage after she became a State; thanks to the
vagabonds, she has extended her boundaries:
for, it is they who, in order to maintain their
independence, fought against the nomad tribes
who attacked them from the south and the
east. . . ."

There is a marked difference between these
two classes: men of the former look for a place
on this earth where they can establish themselves; while men of the other class, those who
are out of work, drunkards, and lazy men, have
no taste for a sedentary life.

But if Gorky has not created the type of
vagabond which is so familiar to those who
know Russian literature, on the other hand, he
has remodeled it with his original, energetic, and
vibrantly realistic talent. His nomad " barefoot brigade," picturesquely encamped, is sur-

rounded with a sort of terribly majestic halo in these vast stretches of country, a background against which their sombre silhouettes are set off. From the perfumed steppes to the roaring sea, they conjure up to the eye of their old co-mate the enchanting Slavic land of which they are the audacious offsprings. And Gorky also lovingly gives them a familiar setting, painted with bold strokes, of plains and mountains which border in the distance the glaucous stretch of the sea. The sea! With what fervor does Gorky depict the anger and the peace of the sea. It always inspires, like an adored mistress:

" . . . The sea sleeps.

" Immense, sighing lazily along the strand, it has gone to sleep, peaceful in its huge stretch, bathed in the moonlight. As soft as velvet, and black, it mingles with the dark southern sky and sleeps profoundly, while on its surface is reflected the transparent tissue of the flaky, immobile clouds, in which is incrusted the gilded design of the stars."

Thus, like a " leitmotiv," the murmuring of the water interrupts the course of the story. And the steppe, this steppe " which has devoured so much human flesh and has drunk so much blood that it has become fat and fecund," surrounds with its immensity these miserable wandering beings and menaces them with its storm:

" Suddenly, the entire steppe undulated, enveloped with a dazzling blue light which seemed to enlarge the horizon . . . the shadows trembled and disappeared for a moment . . . a crash of thunder burst forth, disturbing the sky, where many black clouds were flying past. . . .

" . . . At times the steppe stretched forth like an oscillating giant . . . the vast stretch of blue and cloudless sky poured light down upon us, and seemed like an immense cupola of sombre color."

The wind passed " in large and regular waves, or blew with a sharp rattle, the leaves sighed and whispered among themselves, the waves of the river washed up on the banks, monotonous, despairing, as if they were telling something terribly sad and mournful," the entire country vibrated with a powerful life that harmonized with the souls of the people.

In " Old Iserguile," Gorky writes: " I should have liked to transform myself into dust and be blown about by the wind; I should have liked to stretch myself out on the steppe like the warm waters of the river, or throw myself into the sea and rise into the sky in an opal mist; I should have liked to drink in this evening so wonderful and melancholy. . . . And, I know not why, I was suffering. . . ."

Gorky's stories, always short enough, have little or no plot, and the characters are barely sketched. But, in these simple frames, he has confined the power of an art which is prolific, supple and profoundly living. Let us take, for example, " The Friends." Dancing Foot and The One Who Hopes are ordinary thieves, the terror of the villagers whose gardens they rob. One day, when they are especially desperate, they steal a thin horse which is browsing at the edge of the woods. The One Who Hopes gets an incurable sickness, and it is perhaps on account of his approaching death that he feels scruples at this crime. Dancing Foot expresses the scorn that the weakness of his companion inspires him with, but he ends by giving in and returns the animal. One hour later, The One Who Hopes falls dead in front of Dancing Foot, who is tremendously upset in spite of his affected indifference.

A dry outline cannot possibly convey the emotion contained in this little drama, where the low mentality of the characters is rendered with the mastery which Gorky usually shows in creating his elemental heroes. Among other works that should be noted are " Cain and Arteme," so poignantly ironical in its simplicity, " To Drive Away Tedium," " The Silver Clasps," " The Prisoner," and that little masterpiece, " Twenty-Six Men and a Girl," in which we see twenty-six bakers pouring out an ideal and mystical love on Tanya, the little embroiderer, who they believe, is as pure as an angel. One day, a brutal soldier comes to defy them, and boasts that he will conquer this young girl. He succeeds. Then the twenty-six insult their fallen idol; the tragedy is not so much in the insults that they hurl at her, as in the suffering they undergo through having lost the illusion that was so dear to them.

Let us note, incidentally, the existence of a sort of comic spirit in these works which relieves the tragedy of the situations. In spite of their dark pessimism, the actors in these little dramas have an appearance of gaiety which deceives. It is by this popular humor that Gorky is the continuator of the work of Gogol; this is especially noticeable in " The Fair at Goltva."

In studying Gorky, one is often struck by the homogeneity of the types which he has described. Open any of his books, and you will always meet that " restless " type, dissatisfied with the banality of his existence, trying to get away from it, and leaning irresistibly towards absolute liberty, far removed from social and political obligations.

Who are these " restless " people? Toward what end are they striving? What do they represent? First, they have an immense reserve force which they do not know what to do with; they have got out of the rut, the rut which they despise, but it is hard for them to create another sort of existence for themselves. Bourgeois happiness repulses them, while all sorts of duties are hateful to them. They consider the people who are contented with this sort of a life as slaves, unworthy of the name of man, and they show the same disdain for the peasants, for the leading classes, and for the workingmen. The simple farmer excites the scorn of the " barefoot brigade: "

" As for me," says one of them, " I don't like any peasants. . . . They are all dogs! They have provincial States, and they do for them. . . . They tremble, they are hypocrites, but they want to live; they have one protection: the soil. . . . However, we must tolerate the peasant, for he has a certain usefulness."

" What is a peasant? " asks another. And he answers the question himself: " The peasant is for all men a matter of food, that is to say, an animal that can be eaten. The sun, the water, the air, and the peasant are indispensable to man's existence. . . ."

One might think that this hostility was the fruit of a feeling of envy provoked by the fact that the peasant seems to enjoy so many advantages. But, on the contrary, the " barefoot brigade " admits that the peasant subjugates his individuality for any sort of profit, and that he cannot feel the yoke which he has voluntarily taken in the hope of getting his daily bread.

These workingmen " who pitifully dig in the soil " are unfortunate slaves. " They do nothing but construct, they work perpetually, their blood and sweat are the cement of all the edifices of the earth. And yet the remuneration which they receive, although they are crushed by their work, does not give them shelter or enough food really to live on."

The enlightened classes are always characterized in Gorky's works by violent traits. The architect Shebouyev accords a sufficiently great, but scarcely honorable, place to the category of intelligent men to whom he belongs.

" All of us," he says, " are nonentities, deprived of happiness. We are in such great numbers! And our numbers have been a power for so long a time! We are animated by so many desires, pure and honest. . . . Why is there so much talk among us and so little action? And, all the while, the germs are there! . . . All these papers, novels, articles are germs . . . just germs, and nothing else. . . . Some of us write, others read; after reading, we discuss; after discussing, we forget what we have read. For us, life is tedious, heavy, grey, and burden-

some. We live our lives, but sigh from fatigue
and complain of the heavy burdens we are carrying."

The journalist Yezhov, in " Thomas Gordeyev," expresses himself in the same manner, but
even more decisively:

" I should like to say to the intelligent classes:
' You people are the best in my country! Your
life is paid for by the blood and tears of ten
Russian generations! How much you have cost
your country! And what do you for her?
What have you given to life? What have you
done? . . .' "

The absence of all independence, of any passion even a little sincere, the complete submission of heart and mind to the old prescribed
morality, the constant effort to realize mere
personal ambitions — all of these are the re-
proaches that Gorky addresses to cultivated
man, whose moral disintegration he proves has
been produced by routine and prejudice.

In contrast to them, the vagabonds are the in-
stinctive enemies of all slavery, in any form
whatsoever. The complete independence of
their personality means everything to them.
And no material conditions, no matter how pros-
perous, will induce them to make the least com-
promise on this point. One of these " restless "
types, Konovalov, tells how, after he had bound
himself to the wife of a rich merchant, he could

have lived in the greatest comfort, but he abandoned everything, the easy life, and even the woman, whom he loved well enough, in order to go out and look for the unknown. This is a common adventure on the part of Gorky's heroes.

What is the cause of this restlessness?

" Well, you see," explains Konovalov, " I became weary. It was such weariness, I must tell you, little brother, that at moments I simply could not live. It seemed to me as if I were the only man on the whole earth, and, with the exception of myself, there was no living thing anywhere. And in those moments, everything was repugnant to me, everything in the world; I became a burden to myself, and if everybody were dead, I wouldn't even sigh! It must have been a disease with me, and the reason why I took to drink, for, before this time, I never drank."

For the same reasons, in " Anguish," a workingman leaves his mistress and his employer, the miller. Where does this anguish come from? Perhaps it is the simple result of a psychological process which, Konovalov admits, is nothing other than a disease. It is very possible that, in impulsive acts, a psychiatrist would see something analogous to alcoholism, or the symptoms of some other anomaly.

Turgenev had already analyzed a similar case in " The Madman." When Michael Poltev is asked what evil spirit led him to drink and to risk his life, he always refers to his anguish.

" ' Why this anguish? ' asks his uncle.

" ' Why? . . . When the brain is free, one begins to think of poverty, injustice, Russia. . . . And that's the end! anguish hastens on. . . . One is ready to send a bullet through one's head! There's nothing left to do but get drunk! . . .'

" ' And why do you associate Russia with all of that? Why, you are nothing but a sluggard! '

" ' But I can do nothing, dear uncle! . . . Teach me what I ought to do, to what task I ought to consecrate my life. I will do it gladly! . . .' "

Gorky's characters give the same explanation of their " ennui," and almost in identical terms. This disgust comes in great part from not knowing how to adapt oneself to life, nor how to become a " useful " man.

" Take me, for instance," says Konovalov, " what am I? A vagabond . . . a drunkard, a crack-brained sort of man. There is no reason for my life. Why do I live on earth, and to whom am I useful? I have no home, no wife, no children, and I don't feel as if I wanted any. I live and am bored. . . . What about? No

one knows. I have no life within myself, do
you understand? How shall I express it?
There's a spark, or force lacking in my
soul. . . ."

Another character, the shoemaker Orlov, in
" Orlov and His Wife," especially reflects this
pessimistic disposition. In the same way as
Konovalov, he is born with " restlessness in his
heart."

He is a shoemaker; and why?

" As if there weren't enough of them already!
What pleasure is there in this trade for me? I
sit in a cellar and sew. Then I shall die. They
say that the cholera is coming. . . . And after
that? Gregory Orlov lived, made shoes — and
died of the cholera. What does that signify?
And why was it necessary that I should live,
make shoes and die, tell me? "

These creatures are under the impression that
they are superfluous; therefore their pessimistic
conclusions. All of them pasionately want to be
able to express the meaning of life in general,
their life in particular, but the task is too much
for them.

Gorky's heroes consider themselves " useless
beings," but they never humiliate themselves.
Their restlessness of spirit does not permit them
to resign themselves to the reigning banality or
to take part in it without protesting. At the
same time, some of them are gifted with suf-

ficient personality to possess an unshaken faith in themselves, in their strength, which keeps them from letting the responsibility of their torments fall back upon society.

Promtov, the hero of " The Strange Companion," makes these restless seekers the descendants of the Wandering Jew: " Their peculiarity," he ironically says, " is, that whether rich or poor, they cannot find a suitable place for themselves on earth, and establish themselves in it. The greatest of them are satisfied with nothing: money, women, nor men."

What, then, do these " greatest " want?

Their desires evidently take a multitude of forms, and have the most diverse shades; but the greatest number of them are impatient for extraordinary happenings, eager for exploits. Some of them declare that they would be willing to throw themselves on a hundred knives if humanity could be relieved by their doing so. But simple daily activity, even if it is useful, does not satisfy them.

The shoemaker Orlov leaves his cellar, as he calls it, and accepts a position in the hospital where they are taking care of cholera patients. His devotion makes him an " indispensable man; " he is reborn, and, according to his own words, he is " ripe for life." It seems as if his end were going to be attained. But not so.

Restlessness seizes him again. Orlov questions
the value of his work. He saves sick people
from the cholera. Is he doing good? The
greatest care is taken of these people, but how
many people are there outside of the hospitals,
one hundred times as many as there are inside,
who are just as unfortunate, but, in spite of
that fact, are not helped by any one?

" While you live," he declares, " no one will
refuse to give you a drink of water. And if
you are near death, not only will they not allow
you to die, but they will go to some expense to
stop you. They organize hospitals. . . . They
give you wine at " six and a half rubles a bottle." The sick man gets well, the doctors are
happy, and Orlov would like to share their joy;
but he cannot, for he knows that, on leaving the
threshold of the hospital, a life " worse than the
convulsions of the cholera " awaits the conva-
lescent. . . . And again he is seized by the desire to drink, and to be a vagabond, and by a
wish to experience new sensations.

These, then, are the vagabonds whom we can
class in the category of the " restless." After
these, come those whom the author terms the
" ex-men," and whom he studies, under this title,
in one of his longest stories. The ex-men are
closely related to the " restless; " however, they
differ from them in that they push their opinions

to an extreme, for they are, more than the others,
miserable and at bay against society.

"What difference would it make if it all
went to the devil," one of them philosophizes —
"I should like to see the earth go to pieces suddenly, provided that I should perish the last,
after having seen the others die. . . . I'm an
ex-man, am I not? I am a pariah, then, es-
tranged from all bonds and duties. . . . I can
spit on everything!"

Thomas Gordeyev's father develops another
thesis; a rich and rational bourgeois, he tries
to inculcate in his son from his infancy —
a son who later augments the ranks of the
"restless" — the most perfect spirit of egotism.

"You must pity people," he says, "but do
it with discernment. First, look at a man, see
what good you can get out of him, and see
what he is good for. If you think he is a
strong man, capable of work, help him. But
if you think him weak and little suited for
work, abandon him without pity. Remember
this: two boards have fallen into the mud, one
of them is worm-eaten, the other is sound.
What are you going to do? Pay no attention
to the worm-eaten plank, but take out the sound
one and dry it in the sun. It may be of service
to you or to some one else. . . ."

The reader will note the absolute egotism in

all of Gorky's types. The "restless" are interested only in their own misery, and they think that all men are like them; nor do they try to stop or bridle their passions.

Strong passions are one of the most precious privileges of mankind. This truth is well shown in the story: "Once More About the Devil." [7] Here, the men have become shabby and insignificant since there has been propagated among them, with a new strength, the gospel of individual perfection. The demon stifles, in the heart of Ivan Ivanovich Ivanov, all the passions that can agitate a human soul, — ambition, pity, evil, and anger; this operation makes Ivan an absolutely perfect being. On his face there appears that beatitude which words cannot express. The devil has crushed all "substance" out of him, and he is completely "empty."

One understands that Gorky's heroes cannot find what would be good for them, nor feel the least satisfaction in doing their fellow men a good service. They only dream of action; their sole desire is to affirm their individualty, by "manifesting" themselves, little matter how. Old Iserguille is persuaded that "in life, there is room for mighty deeds" and, if a man likes them, he will find occasion to do them. Konovalov is most enthusiastic over Zhermak,[8] to whom he feels himself akin.

" I'd like to reduce the whole earth to dust,"
dreams Orlov, " or get up a crowd of comrades
and kill off all the Jews . . . all, to the very
last one! Or, in general, do something that
would place me high above all men, so that I
could spit on them from up there, and cry to
them: ' Dogs! Why do you live? You're all
hypocritical rascals and nothing more. . . .' "

These people demand a boundless liberty, but
how obtain it? All of them dream of a certain
organization which will let them feel relieved
of all their duties, of all the thousands of petty
things that make life hard, of all the small details, conventions, and obligations which hold
such an important place in our society. But
the time for heroic deeds has passed away, and
the " restless " fight in vain against the millions
of men who are determined to keep their habits
and advantages.

Thus they are obliged to shake the dust off
their feet and to leave the ranks in which they
are suffocating. No matter what they do or
what they try to do, their motto is, " each one
for himself."

" Come," says a vagabond poetically to
Thomas Gordeyev, " come with me on the open
road, into the fields and steppes, across the
plains, over the mountains, come out and look
at the world in all its freedom. The thick
forests begin to murmur; their sweet voice

praises divine wisdom; God's birds sing its glory and the grass of the steppe burns with the incense of the Holy Virgin.

" The soul is filled with an ardent yet calm joy, you desire nothing, you envy no one. . . . And it is then that it seems as if on the whole earth there is no one but God and you. . . ."

The material inconveniences of such an existence hardly affect Gorky's characters. Promtov, one of the prophets of individualism, says, in speaking of himself:

" I have been ' on the road ' for ten years, and I have not complained of my fate to God. I don't want to tell you anything of this period, because it is too tedious. . . . In general, it is the joyous life of a bird. Sometimes, grain is lacking, but one must not be too exacting and one must remember that kings themselves do not have pleasures only. In a life like ours, there are no duties — that is the first pleasure — and there are no laws, except those of nature — that is the second. Without a doubt, the gentlemen of the police force bother one at times . . . but you find fleas even in the best hotels. As a set-off, one can go to the right, or to the left, or straight ahead, wherever your heart bids you go, and if you don't want to go anywhere, after having provided yourself with bread from the hut of some peasant, who will never refuse it, you can lie down until you care to resume your travels. . . ."

This is the final point at which all of the " restless " arrive, believing that there they will find what they have always lacked. Even the author himself shares their views up to a certain point:

" You have to be born in civilized society," he says, speaking of himself, " in order to have the patience to live there all your life without having the desire to flee from this circle, where so many restrictions hinder you, restrictions sanctioned by the habit of little poisoned lies, this sickly center of self-love, in one word, all this vanity of vanities which chills the feelings and perverts the mind, and which is called in general, without any good reason and very falsely, civilization.

" I was born and brought up outside of it, and I am glad of that fact. Because of it, I have never been able to absorb culture in large doses, without feeling, at the end of a certain time, the terrible need of stepping out of this frame. . . . It does one good to go into the dens of the cities, where everything is dirty, but simple and sincere; or even to rove in the fields or on the highroads; one sees curious things there. It refreshes the mind; and all you need in order to do it is a pair of sturdy legs. . . ."

What then is the teaching that we get out of
Gorky's works? For, faithful to Russian tradition, he does not practise art for art's sake.
His " barefoot brigade " and his " restless "
men are generally considered as representative
of his own ideals. The principle of " Do what
seems to you to be good " — a principle which
is expressed by a wandering and free life —
ought to be justified, one thinks. Critics have
risen up against this ideal, trying to prove how
incompatible the kind of existence that he conceives is with a solid political organization, and
how far from reality the men are whom he represents.

Doubtless, in real life, people are not as
original and not as heroic as Gorky represents
them to be. And he himself agrees that their
inventive faculties are very highly developed.
He shows this in putting the following words
into the mouth of Promtov:

" I have very probably exaggerated, but
that's not of much importance. For, if I have
exaggerated what happened, my method of ex-
position has shown the true state of my soul.
Perhaps, I have served you with an imaginary
roast, but the sauce is made of the purest
truth."

The end that he is after, Gorky has shown us
in his story, " The Lecturer," which contains
his theories on literature. In the person of the

lecturer, he addresses himself to the men who represent the majority of the Russian cultivated classes. He begins by analyzing himself carefully and discovers in himself many good feelings and honest desires, but he feels that he lacks clear and harmonious thought, a thing which keeps all the manifestations of life in equilibrium. Numerous doubts torment him, and his mind has been so moved with them, his heart so wounded, that, for a long time, he has lived " empty inside."

" What have I to say to others? " he asks himself. " That which was told them long ago, that which has always been told them, none of which makes any one any better. But have I the right to teach these ideas and convictions, if I, who was brought up according to them, act so often in opposition to them?

With his usual sincerity, it is not to be wondered at that he answered this question in the negative, and, to cite the words of one of his characters, that he " refused to live in the chains which had already been forged for free thought, and to class himself under the label of an ism."

He has not thought it profitable to hide his doubts and has not feared to declare openly that none of the existing philosophies suit him, and that he is trying to follow his own path. All of his work is but the absolute image of his own uncertainties, of his passionate researches, and of his constant " restlessness."

At times people have believed that he was a disciple of Nietzsche. And, in truth, he has come under his influence, like so many other Russian authors. But he has gone on mostly by himself, aided by his acute sensibility, which has not, as yet, allowed him to adopt any one system to the exclusion of all others, or to formulate a system for his personal use.

" I know one thing,". he says, " it is not happiness that we should hope for. What should we do with it? The meaning of life does not lie in the search for happiness, and the satisfaction of the material appetites will never suffice to make a man fully contented with himself. It is in beauty that we must look for the meaning of life, and in the energy of the will! Every moment of our lives ought to be devoted to some better end. . . ."

However, he has very neatly set forth what he considers the task of the author. According to him, the man of to-day has lost courage; he interests himself too little in life, his desire to live with dignity has grown weaker, " an odor of putrefaction surrounds him, cowardice and slavery corrupt his heart, laziness binds his hands and his mind." But, at the same time, life grows in breadth and depth, and, from day to day, men are learning to question. And it is the writer who ought to answer their questions; but he should not content himself with straightening out the balance sheet of social deterioration, and in giving photographs of daily life. The writer must also awaken in the hearts of men a desire for liberty, and speak energetically, in order to infuse in man an ardent desire to create other forms of life. . . . " It seems to me," says Gorky, " that we desire new dreams, gracious inventions, unforeseen things, because the life which we have created is poor, dreary, and tedious. The reality which formerly we wanted so ardently, has frozen us and broken us down. . . . What is there to do? Let us try: perhaps invention and imagination will aid man in raising himself so that he may again glance for a moment at the place which he has lost on earth."

All of Gorky's characters curse life, but without ceasing to love it, because they " have the taste for life." Their complaints are only a means by which the author hopes to raise up around him " that revengeful shame and the taste for life " of which he so often speaks. Here is the artful Mayakine, who, indignant at the debasement of the younger generation, is ready to take the most cruel means in order " to infuse fire into the veins " of his contemporaries. Varenka Olessova, the heroine of a story, incessantly repeats that people would be more interesting if they were more animated, if they laughed, played, sang more, if they were more audacious, stronger, and even more coarse and vulgar. Gorky admires also the beautiful type, vigorous, with a rudimentary mentality, which meets with his approval simply because he sees in it a nature which is complete, untouched, and filled with a love of life.

Gorky suffers miseries inherent in the mere fact of existence, but he has found no remedy; he looks for consolations in the cult of beauty, in the strength of free individuality, in the flight towards a superior ideal. But he does not know where to find this superior ideal, which vivifies everything. This is perhaps the reason why people have thought they saw in his work the Nietzschean influence, which praises an insistence on individuality in defiance of current conventions, and gives us just as vague a solution as Gorky does.

But this enthusiasm for an ideal, vague as it is, this passionate appeal for energy in the struggle, has awakened powerful echoes in the hearts of the Russians, especially the younger of them. Gorky suddenly became their favorite author, and it is to this warm reception that he owes a great part of his renown. He has carried the young along with him, and they have put their ideals in the place which he had left empty.

If we now pass on to the first novels and
dramas of Gorky, we shall be struck by the
fact that, in spite of the talent shown in them,
they are very inferior to his short stories. His
former mastery is not found, except in his later
novels, which we shall take occasion to mention
presently.

" Thomas Gordeyev " contains some very
fine passages, but is not very successful as a
whole. Thomas's father is a merchant on the
banks of the Volga; he is an energetic man who
carries out all his ideas. Whatever he is engaged on, whether business affairs, or a debauch,
or repentance thereof, he gives himself entirely
to the impression of the moment. Like other
men of his class, moreover, he lives a life which
is a singular mixture of refinement and savagery.
He spends his time in drinking and working, as
much for himself as for his only son, Thomas,
whose mother died in giving birth to him. The
child grows up under the care of his aunt and
shows a serious disposition toward study.
Gradually, he feels the motives that make men
act, and he questions his father about them.

Before dying, the latter says to his son:
" Don't count on men, don't count on great
events." In spite of the wealth which he in-
herits Thomas is not happy; he has no friends;
his colleagues, the merchants, and especially his
father's old friend, Mayakine, are repulsive to

him on account of their cupidity and their un-
scrupulousness. Thomas does not love money
and does not understand its power, two things
that people cannot forgive him for. Besides,
he does not know how to make use of the forces
that are burning within him. After having
vainly sought for moral relief in debauchery,
he ends by proposing to strike a bargain with
Mayakine so that he can be freed from responsibility and go out and look for happiness. He
will give Mayakine his personal fortune if the
latter will look after his business affairs. But
the old roué, who hopes to get possession of
the fortune in a surer way, refuses, and their
conversation turns into a quarrel.

As he does not work, Thomas indulges in
many extravagances in company with a journalist of very advanced ideas. Finally, one day
when he is at a fête at which are present all
the wealthy members of the merchant class, the
young man, disgusted with their vices, rises to
apostrophize them in the most bitter terms.
They throw themselves on him, and he is arrested as a madman and put into an asylum.
He comes out, only to abandon himself to drink.

In " The Three," Gorky tells us the life
story of Ilya Lounyev, a poor creature, born
in poverty, whose life is full of deceptions, misfortunes, even crimes. Several times, Ilya has
tried to lead a decent life; but it is his sincerity

that makes him lose his position with the merchant for whom he works. He has believed in beauty and in the purity of love, and he is deceived by the woman he loves. Gradually all the baseness of the world becomes clear to him. In a moment of jealousy he kills his mistress's lover, an old miser. Several months later he publicly confesses his crime, and, in order to escape from human justice, he commits suicide.

In his first two dramas, " The Smug Citizen," and " A Night's Refuge," as in his short stories, Gorky shows us his usual characters.

The Bessemenovs, comfortable, petty bourgeois, have given their children an education. Their daughter, Tatyana, becomes a school-teacher, but her profession does not please her. Peter, their son, has been expelled from the university, in spite of his indifference toward " new " ideas. The children are continually harassed by their father, who bemoans the fact that he has given them an education. Besides, another sadness troubles him: Nil, his adopted son, whom he has had taught the trade of a mechanician, — an alert and industrious fellow, — wants to marry Polya, a girl without a fortune. The father is beside himself, for, if Nil marries, he will never be in a condition to pay back the money that has been spent on him. But Nil protests: he is young, and, some day,

he will repay his debt. He has not noticed that
Tatyana is in love with him; and the young
girl has not strength enough to live through
the sorrow of seeing herself abandoned forever.
She tries to commit suicide, but does not succeed. While Tatyana is bemoaning her fate,
Peter has fallen in love with a young woman
quite different from any of the members of his
family. Helen understands how sad Peter's
position is among these ignorant people, and
she decides to marry him, for pity as much as
for love. The father is no more satisfied with
this match than he was with Nil's, and with
death in his soul he is present at the dismember-
ment of his family. While Helen takes Peter,
Nil goes off with Polya. The mother, a humble
and kind woman, does not understand the cause
of all this dissension and, while consoling the
weeping Tatyana, she asks her husband: "Why
are our children punishing us so? Why do
they make us suffer?" This play is not dra-
matically effective and has never had a great
success on the stage.

On the other hand, Gorky's second attempt,
"A Night's Refuge," has been enormously successful. Here, the author takes us into the
world of the barefoot brigade. Vasska Pepel,
Vassilissa's lover, the proprietor of the night
refuge in which he sleeps, loves the sister
of his mistress, Natasha by name, a timid and

dreamy young girl, who blooms like a lily in this mire. The old vagabond, Luke, advises the young girl to run off with Vasska, who wants to begin a new life. But Vassilissa, jealous and evil as she is, has noticed the coldness which her lover shows towards her. She avenges herself by striking her younger sister whenever she can. Her plan was, with the aid of Vasska, to kill her husband, Kostylev, and then to live openly with her lover. But when she sees Vasska ready to leave with Natasha, she starts a terrible scene, which ends in Vasska's killing Kostylev without meaning to. Vassilissa and her lover are arrested and Natasha disappears.

Although the characters of this play are vagabonds, they differ from most of Gorky's creations, whose fiery and enthusiastic souls usually discover a real beauty in the life they have chosen. Alcoholism, prostitution, and misery have shut off these people who live in the cellar. They have fallen so low, that conscience is a useless luxury for them. It belongs to the rich only. One of them, who is asked if he has a conscience, replies with sincere astonishment: " What? Conscience? " And when the question is asked again, he answers, " What good is conscience? I'm not a rich man." The life of these people is worse than a nightmare: to-morrow they will be cold, hungry, and drunk, just as they were yesterday. Sometimes, perhaps, they feel like struggling against their evil lot, but no one stretches forth a helping hand to them. They do not dare think of the future, and they would like to forget the past. One of them expresses his fear of life thus:

" At times, I'm afraid, brother; can you understand that? . . . I tremble. . . . For, what is there after this? " And this fear smothers all the energy in them. They are poor and scantily clothed, not only in the material sense of the word, but also in the moral sense. Money would not be necessary to save them, but a word of sympathy, of love, a word that would give them the courage really to live.

And it is here that old Luke appears. He treats the men as if they were children, and gains their confidence. In his words there is manifested a real experience of things and people. As he says, " They moulded me a lot," and that is why he became " tender." He knows just the right word for every one. He assures the dying woman that: " Eternal rest means happiness. Die, and you will have rest, you will have no cares, and no one to fear. Silence will calm you! All you have to do is remain lying down! Death pacifies and is tender. You will appear before God, and He will say to you: ' Take her to Paradise so that she may rest. I know that her life has been hard; she is tired, give her peace.' " And the sick woman, who has dragged out her existence so long, is consoled.

To the drunkard, a former actor who has fallen, Luke says: " Stop drinking, pull yourself together and be patient. You will be cured, and you will begin a new existence. . . ." And he succeeds in awakening a hope of a better life in the soul of the poor comedian, while he himself, perhaps, hardly believes in the possible regeneration of his protégé.

After Luke's departure, the temporary dreams of these miserable people vanish. One evening, when they are all gathered around a bottle of brandy, they strike up a song. A friend, a baron by birth, rushes into the cellar and announces that the actor has hung himself, and that his corpse is hanging in the court. A deathlike silence follows these words. All look at each other in fright. " Ah, the fool! " finally murmurs a vagabond, " he spoiled our song. . . ." The hope in a better life that Luke had awakened in the actor made him kill himself, when he saw that he had not enough strength to realize this hope.

This drama is the quintessence of all that Gorky has, up to this time, written on the " ex-man," whom he has thoroughly " explored." And the figure of old Luke is one of his most original and lifelike creations.

His third important play, which, however,

has never enjoyed the popularity of " A Night's Refuge," is called: " The Children of the Sun." The " children of the sun " are the elect of heaven, richly endowed with talent and knowledge. They live in a world of noble dreams, of elevated thoughts, enveloped though they are in the greyness of life. There pass before them long processions of tired and oppressed people. The latter, also, have been generated by the strong sun; but the light has gone out for them, and they travel on life's highway without joy or faith, among those who are proud of their beauty or learning. The " children of the sun " are the aristocrats of the soul. They have but one end: to make life beautiful, good, and agreeable for all. They continually think of making it easier, of soothing suffering, and of preparing a better future. Their mission is a large one. They are not idle, but are men who have the most elevated ends in view.

Between " the children of the sun " and " the children of the earth " there is a deep abyss. They do not understand each other. The " children of the sun " cannot admit the miseries and ugliness of daily life. They have compassion for the people who work below them. The " children of the earth " feel the superiority of the " children of the sun," but their narrow-mindedness, continually absorbed by the necessity of finding shelter and food, cannot rise to

the preoccupations of so elevated an order.
However, life brings these two worlds together
in a common work; but their mere meeting on
the ground of practical interests produces a
collision.

A third category constitutes the intermediary
link. This is made up of the university people,
the representatives of the liberal professions.
As " intellectuals," they cannot equal the " children of the sun," but they can understand them.
They conceive the grandeur of their moral activity. At the same time, these men are close to
the people. They are often obliged to mingle
in the life of the people, and more than the
" children of the sun," they are capable of enlarging their minds and ennobling their duties.
But, while they know and understand the duties
of the people completely, they are not yet strong
enough to help them. This, then, is the general
meaning of the play.

Although this play is cleverly constructed,
with a last act which is pathetic and moving in
its intensity, and produces a profound impression, on the whole, unfortunately, it has the
general harshness of problem plays. Under its
lyric vestments, its solid and massive character
appears too often. Gorky, a born observer,
inheritor of the realistic traditions of his country, could not help turning aside, one day, from

this ideological art, visibly influenced by Tolstoy's dramas. The direct part that the romanticist has played in the political events of his country sufficiently proves that he has taken a different road from that taken by the apostle of Yasnaya Polyana. With maturity, he felt the need of hastening the dénouement of the crisis in Russia, in actively participating in its emancipation. From that time on, he chose his heroes from a less singular environment. Instead of the philosophic vagabonds, the neurasthenic " restless " ones, and the ex-men, he chose the plebeian of the city and country, who is gradually awakening from a sleep of ignorance and slavery. A remarkable story, called " In Prison," all atremble with new sensations, inaugurates this new style. A victim himself of the intolerance of " over-men," Gorky has incarnated his own revolts and hopes in the soul of his hero, Misha, a brother of the revolutionary students who do not hesitate to sacrifice their life or liberty for a principle or ideal.

Written at the same time, the story called " The Soldiers " gives proof of an equally careful incorporation of the claims of the oppressed in a literary work.

The school-mistress, Vera, has conceived the daring project of teaching the soldiers who are quartered in the village. She gets some of them together at the edge of the neighboring woods and there she tries to show them the ignominy of the rôles they play in times of uprisings. Angered by this unexpected talk, the soldiers threaten the young girl. But her coolness and sincerity finally make them listen to her with a respect mingled with admiration.

A third story, called "Slaves," in a masterful way retraces the catastrophes of the now historical journey of January 9, 1905, at the end of which, a crowd of 200,000 men, led by the famous pope Gapon, went to the Tsar's palace to present their demands to him, and were received with cannon shots.

These stories were followed by three works of great merit: "Mother," "A Confession," and "The Spy."

The novel "Mother" takes us into the midst of revolutionary life. The heroes of this book belong, for the most part, to that workingman and agricultural proletariat whose rôle has lately been of such great importance in the Russian political tempests. With marvelous psychological analysis, Gorky shows how some of these simple creatures understand the new truth, and how it gradually penetrates their ardent souls.

Pavel Vlassov, a young, intelligent workingman, is thirsty for knowledge, and is the apostle of the new ideal. He throws himself heart and soul into the dangerous struggle he has undertaken against ignorance and oppres-

sion. The Little Russian, Andrey, is all feeling and thought, and the peasant Rybine is in-
flamed by action. Sashenka is a young girl
who sacrifices herself entirely to the Idea, and
the coal-man Ignatius is driven by an obscure
force to help in a cause which he does not understand. Finest of them all is Pelaguaya
Vlassov, the principal character of the book,
and Pavel's mother.

Old and grey, Pelaguayá has passed her
whole life in misery. She has never known anything but how to suffer in silence and endure
without complaint; she has never dreamed that
life could be different. One day her father had
said to her:

" It's useless to make faces! There is a fool
who wants to marry you, — take him. All girls
marry, all women have children; children are,
for all parents, a sorrow. And are you, yes or
no, a human being? "

She then marries the workingman Michael
Vlassov, who gets drunk every day, beats her
cruelly and kicks her, and even on his death-bed,
says: " Go to the devil. . . . Bitch! I'll die
better alone."

He dies, and his son Pavel begins to bring forbidden books into the house. Friends come and
talk; a small group is formed. Pelaguaya
listens to what is said, but understands nothing.
Gradually, however, there begins to filter into

her old breast, like a stream of joy, an understanding of something big, of something in
which she can take part. She discovers that
she too is a free creature, and, obscurely, there
is formed in her mind the notion that every
human being has a right to live. Then she
speaks: " The earth is tired of carrying so
much injustice and sadness, it trembles softly
at the hope of seeing the new sun which is
rising in the bosom of mankind." So the obscure and miserable woman gradually rises to
the dignity of " The Mother of the Prophet."
And when Pavel accepts, like the martyrdom
of the cross, his banishment to Siberia, with
a joyous heart she sacrifices her son to the
Idea.

Her soul opens wide to the new truth that is
lighting it. With the most touching abnega-
tion, she tries to carry on the work of the ab-
sent one. But the police are watching. One
day, when she is about to take the train to a
neighboring town to spread the " good word "
there, she is recognized and apprehended. Seeing that she is lost, the Mother, whose personality at this moment grows absolutely symbolic,
cries out to the crowd:

" ' Listen to me! They condemned my son
and his friends because they were bringing the
truth to everybody! We are dying from work,
we are tormented by hunger and by cold, we

are always in the mire, always in the wrong!
Our life is a night, a black night!'

" ' Hurrah for the old woman!' cries some
one in the crowd.

" A policeman struck her in the chest; she
tottered, and fell on the bench. But she still
cried:

" ' All of you! get all your forces together
under a single leader.'

" The big red hand of the policeman struck
her in the throat, and the nape of her neck hit
against the wall.

" ' Shut up, you hag!' cried the officer in a
sharp voice.

" The Mother's eyes grew larger and shone
brightly. Her jaw trembled.

" ' They won't kill a resurrected soul!'

" ' Bitch!'

" With a short swing the policeman struck
her full in the face.

" Something red and black momentarily
blinded the Mother; blood filled her mouth.

" A voice from the crowd brought her to
herself:

" ' You haven't the right to strike her!'

" But the officers pushed her, and hit her on
the head.

" ' . . . It's not blood that will drown what's
right.' . . .

" Dulled and weakened, the Mother tottered.

But she saw many eyes about her, glowing with
a bold fire, eyes that she knew well and that
were dear to her.

" ' . . . They will never get at the truth,
even under oceans of blood! '

" The policeman seized her heavily by the
throat.

" There was a rattling in her throat:

" . . . ' The unfortunates! '

" Some one in the crowd answered her, with
a deep sigh."

" A Confession " is the story of a restless
soul who untiringly searches for the God of
truth and goodness. Found as a child in a
village of central Russia, Matvey was first
taken by a sacristan, and, after his death, by
Titov, the inspector of the domain. In order
to debase Matvey, whose superiority irritates
him, Titov asks him to participate in his ex-
tortions. Having become the son-in-law of his
adopted father, Matvey, on account of his love
for his wife, accepts the shameful life. But the
God in whom Matvey has placed his distracted
confidence, seems to want to chastise him cruelly.
After having lost, one after the other, his wife
and child, he goes away at a venture. He
enters a monastery where, among the dissolute
monks, whose vices are most repugnant, his
soul gradually shakes off the Christian dogma.

On one of his pilgrimages, he gets to Damascus.
Among the workingmen, where chance has taken
him, he feels his heart opening to the truth,
which he follows up with the determination of
a real Gorkyan hero. The life of the people
appears to him in its sublime simplicity. And
it is in the midst of a dazzling apotheosis —
which reminds one of the most grandiose pages
of Zola's "Lourdes" — that he finally confesses the God of his ideal: it is the people.

"People! you are my God, creator of all
the gods that you have formed from the beauty
of your soul, in your troubled and laborious
search!

"Let there be no other gods on the earth but
yourself, for you are the only God, the creator
of miracles!"

"The Spy" is a study of the Russian police.
The novel treats of the terrible Okhrana, whose
mysterious affairs have become the laughing-
stock of all the foreign papers.

The principal character, about whom circle
the police spies and secret agents, is a poor
orphan, weak and timid, called Evsey Klimkov,
whom his uncle, the forger Piotr, has taken into
his house and brought up with his son, the
strong and brutal James. Beaten by his
schoolmates and by his cousin, the child lives

in a perpetual trance. Life seems formidable
to him, like a jungle in which men are the pitiless beasts. Everywhere, brute force or hypoc-
risy triumph; everywhere, the weak are oppressed, downtrodden, conquered. And in his
feverish imagination, daily excited by facts
which his terror distorts, Evsey delights in con-
ceiving another existence, all made of love and
goodness, an existence that he unceasingly op-
poses against the hard realities of daily life,
with the stubborn fervor of a mystic.

Having entered the service of the old book-
seller Raspopov, the young man does his duty
with the faithfulness of a beast of burden. His
home no longer pleases him at all; there, things
and people are still hostile to him; but his uncle
Piotr seems enchanted with his new position.
Evsey spends his days in arranging and clas-
sifying the books which his master has bought.
A young woman, Raïssa Petrovna, keeps house
for the book-dealer, and as every one knows,
they live like man and wife. In this queer environment, the faculties of the young man become sharpened, and serve him well. It does
not take long for him to find out what they are
hiding from him. A few words addressed by
Raspopov to a certain Dorimedonte Loukhine
reveal to Evsey the part that is being played
by his patron. Raspopov, who is an agent of
the secret police, gives Dorimedonte — who, by

the way, is deceiving him with Raïssa — the
names of the buyers of the forbidden books in
which he trades. And here it is that the tragedy suddenly breaks forth.

Raïssa, tired of being tormented by Raspopov, who accuses her of poisoning him,
strangles the old man in a moment of cold anger, under the very eyes of Evsey. Thanks
to Dorimedonte, this crime goes unpunished.
Evsey, having become the lodger of the two
lovers, now enters the Okhrana, at the advice
of his new master. After a while, Raïssa,
haunted by remorse, commits suicide, and Dorimedonte is killed by some revolutionists.

All the interest of the book, however, is cen-
tered in the picture of the police institutions.
From the chief Philip Philipovich to the agent
Solovyev, Gorky presents, with consummate art,
the mass of corrupt and greedy agents who
wearily accomplish their tasks.

Among them, young Evsey leads a miserable
and ridiculous existence. Bruised by an invincible power, he sees himself compelled to arrest an old man who has confided his revolutionary ideas to him; then a young girl with
whom he is in love; finally, his own cousin, a
revolutionary suspect.

Gradually his eyes are opened. He realizes
that he cannot extricate himself from the position in which he has placed himself. Tired of

leading a life which his conscience disapproves of, he thinks of killing his superior, who has driven him to do so many infamous deeds. He will thus get justice. His project miscarries; maddened, he throws himself under a passing train.

These three remarkable works, riddled by the Russian censor, so that the complete version has appeared only abroad, have recently been followed by two important stories: " Among the People " and " Matvey Kozhemyakine."

With his accustomed power, Gorky shows us, in the first of these stories, the spread of socialism among the agricultural proletariat. He depicts village life with its pettiness and ignominy. The village is for the most part a backward place, hostile to everything that makes a breach in tradition. The hatching of socialism goes on slowly. From day to day, new obstacles, helped on by the ignorance of the peasants, hinder those who are trying to carry out their belief. Even the village guard, Semyon, pursues them with his hatred.

But Igor Petrovich, the propagator of these new ideas, finds, in a few old friends and in a village woman who becomes his mistress, some precious helpers. Thanks to them, he gradually gets up a little circle of firm believers who gather in a cave in the woods. Every evening, they read, discuss, and dream of a better organization, out there in the cave. All would have gone well, if some of them had not betrayed the leader to the police. While being led to the city prison, the leader spoke to the soldiers who were escorting him:

"The soldiers trembled as they clicked their bayonets; they silently listened to the legend of the generous earth which loves those who work it. Again, their red faces were covered with drops of melted snow; the drops ran down their cheeks like bitter tears of humiliation; they breathed heavily, they snuffled, and I felt that they kept walking a little faster, as if they wanted this very day to arrive in that fairy land.

"We are no longer prisoners and soldiers; we are simply seven Russians. I do not forget the prison, but when I remember all that I lived through that summer and before that, my heart fills with joy, and I feel like crying out:

"Rejoice, beloved Russian people! Your resurrection is close at hand!"

"Matvey Kozhemyakine" very brilliantly returns to Gorky's early manner. In this book no symbolic character interprets the bold thoughts of the author. It is simply a novel of Russian provincial life. Its simplicity does not exclude vigor, and it reminds us at times of Balzac.

Young Matvey is the son of an old working-man who has become rich, thanks to his energy and dishonesty. He has grown up in a large house, adjoining a rope-yard, with his father and several servants. His mother, whom he never knew, left home shortly after his birth, and entered a convent in order to escape the torments of life. Later, Matvey's father marries a young girl, in order to provide a mother for his son, whom he loves dearly. But his new mother is not long in finding out the dreary life which she has to lead with the old man. In order to escape from the tedium of it, she listens to the interesting experiences of the wandering life of the porter Sazanov, and gives her unfaithful love in exchange.

Unexpected circumstances disclose this shameful adultery to Matvey. Instead of revealing it to his father, he generously guards the secret. He even goes so far as to protect her from the fury of a workingman, named Savka, whom Sazanov's success has rendered bold. Through gratitude, and later through love, in the absence of Kozhemyakine, she becomes the mistress of her step-son. On his return, the father, finding out about this " liaison," spares his son, but beats his wife to death, and himself, mad with fury, falls, struck with apoplexy.

All the newspapers in the world have attacked Gorky's way of living. As he is forced to remain away from his beloved country, the great writer has made his home in the little island of Capri, the air of which is propitious to his failing health. Moreover, its impressive scenery inspires his restless genius.

Drunk with liberty, taken up with beauty, always ready to help a man who is in political and social difficulties, Gorky, from the depths of his peaceful retreat, wanders out over the world of ideas in search of truth, as formerly he used to wander over the earth in search of bread.

VI

LEONID ANDREYEV

LEONID ANDREYEV was born of a humble bourgeoise family in Orel, in 1871. " It was there that I began my studies," he says. " I was not a good pupil; in the seventh form I was last in my class for a whole year, and I had especially poor reports as to my deportment. The most agreeable part of my schooling, which I still remember with pleasure, was the intervals between the lessons, the ' recesses,' and the times, rare as they were, when the instructor sent me from the class-room for inattention or lack of respect. In the long deserted halls a sonorous silence reigned which vibrated at the solitary noise of my steps; on all sides the closed doors, shutting in rooms full of pupils; a sunbeam — a free beam — played with the dust which had been raised during recess and which had not yet had time to settle; all of it was mysterious, interesting, full of a particular and secret meaning."

Andreyev's father, who was a geometrician,

died while he was still at school, and the family
was without resources.   The young man did
not hesitate, however, in setting out for St.
Petersburg, where he entered the university,
hoping to gain a livelihood by giving lessons.
But it was hard to secure what he wanted.   " I
knew what terrible misery was," Andreyev tells
us; " during my first years in St. Petersburg
I was hungry more than once, and sometimes
I did not eat for two days."

His first literary productions date from this
sombre epoch.   Andreyev gives us remarkably
graphic details of this misery.   One day, he
gave a daily paper a story about the tribula-
tions of an every-hungry student: his own life!
" I wept like a child in writing these pages,"
he confesses.   " I had put down all of my sufferings.   I was still affected by my great sadness when I took the manuscript to the editor.
I was told to come back in a few weeks to find
out whether it had been accepted.   I returned
with a light heart, keeping down my anguish
in expectation of the decision.   It came to me
in the form of a loud burst of laughter from
the editor, who declared that my work was absolutely worthless. . . ."

Nevertheless, he energetically pursued his
studies, which he completed at the University
of Moscow.   " There," he tells us, " life was,
from a material standpoint, less unbearable;

my friends and the aid society came to my
assistance; but I recall my life at the University of St. Petersburg with genuine pleasure;
the various classes of students are there more
differentiated and an individual can more easily
find a sympathetic surrounding among such
distinct groups."

Some time after that, Andreyev, disgusted
with life, attempted suicide. " In January,
1894," he writes, " I tried to shoot myself, but
without any appreciable result. I was punished
by religious penance, imposed upon me by authority, and a sickness of the heart which, although not dangerous, was persistent. During
this time I made one or two equally unsuccess-
ful literary attempts, and I gave myself up
with success to painting, which I have loved
since childhood; I then painted portraits to
order for from 5 to 10 rubles. . . .

" In 1897, I received my counsellor's degree
and I took up that profession in Moscow. For
want of time I did not succeed in getting any
sort of a ' clientele '; in all, I pleaded but one
civil case, which, however, I lost completely,
and several gratuitous criminal cases. However, I was actively working in reporting these
cases for an important paper."

Finally, two strangely impressionistic stories:
" Silence," and " He Was . . . ," published in
an important Petersburg review, brought the

author into prominence. From that time, he
devoted himself entirely to literature.

Andreyev is considered, to-day, as one of the
most brilliant representatives of the new con-
stellation of Russian writers, in which he takes
a place immediately next to Tchekoff, whom he
resembles in the melancholy tone of his work.
In him, as in Tchekoff, the number of people
who suffer from life, either crushed or mutilated by it, by far exceed the number of happy
ones; moreover, the best of his stories are short
and sketchy like those of Tchekoff. Andreyev
is then, so to speak, his spiritual son. But he
is a sickly son, who carries the melancholy element to its farthest limit. The grey tones of
Tchekoff have, in Andreyev, become black; his
rather sad humor has been transformed into
tragic irony; his subtle impressionability into
morbid sensibility. The two writers have had
the same visions of the anomalies and the horrors
of existence; but, where Tchekoff has only a
disenchanted smile, Andreyev has stopped, dis-
mayed; the sensation of horror and suffering
which springs from his stories has become an
obsession with him; it does not penetrate merely
the souls of his heroes, but, as in Poe, it penetrates even the descriptions of nature.

Thus, the " near and terrible " disk of the
moon hovers over the earth like the " gigantic

menace of an approaching but unknown evil ";
the river congeals in " mute terror," and silence
is particularly menacing. Night always comes
" black and bad," and fills human hearts with
shadows. When it falls, the very branches of
the trees " contract, filled with terror." Under
the influence of the disturbing sounds of the
tocsin, the high linden-trees " suddenly begin to
talk, only to become quiet again immediately
and lapse into a sullen silence." The tocsin itself is animated. " Its distinct tones spread
with rapid intensity. Like a herald of evil who
has not the time to look behind him, and whose
eyes are large with fright, the tocsin desperately calls men to the fatal mire." [9]

Most of Andreyev's characters, like those of
Dostoyevsky, are abnormal, madmen and neur-
asthenics in whom are distinguishable marked
traces of degeneration and psychic perversion.
They are beings who have been fatally wounded
in their life-struggle, whose minds now are completely or partially powerless. Too weak to
fight against the cruel exigencies of reality,
they turn their thoughts upon themselves and
naturally arrive at the most desolate conclusions, and commit the most senseless acts.
Some, a prey to the mania of pride, despairing
because of their weakness and their " nothingness," look — as does Serge Petrovich —
for relief in suicide. Others, who have resigned

themselves to their sad lives, become passive
observers, become transformed into living
corpses whose sole desire is peace; such a one
is the hero of " At the Window." Others still
instinctively choke in themselves the best tendencies of their characters and are passionately
fond of futile and senseless amusements, by
means of which they enjoy themselves like children, until a catastrophe makes them " come
back to themselves." This is the idea of the
original story called " The Grand Slam." In
" The Lie " Andreyev depicts the pathological
process in the soul of a man who, crushed by the
falsehood of his own solitary existence, becomes
insane at the idea that truth is inaccessible to
human reason and that the reign of the Lie is
invincible. The hero of " The Thought " [10]
reveres but one thing in the world — his own
thought. Wrapped up in this one idea, he admires the force and finesse of it, while his reason, detached from reality and having only
him for an end, begins to weaken, becomes
gradually perverted to the point where this
man, harassed by a terrible doubt, begins to ask
himself whether he is insane. In the long and
pathetic story, " The Life of a Priest," we are
shown the disturbance of the religious feelings
of a country priest who, although he has an
ardent and strong soul, is crushed by his moral
isolation among the ignorant people of a miser-

able village. It is again this moral isolation
that is analyzed in " Silence," in which story
it is the cause of a domestic tragedy. The
same cause provokes a rupture between a father
and a son in " The Obscure Distance," and
brings with it in some way the death of the
neurasthenic student.

In general, the stories of Andreyev, after
passing through various catastrophes, lead the
reader back to this theme, — the moral isolation of a human being, who feels that the world
has become deserted, and life a game of
shadows. The abyss which separates Andreyev's heroes from other men makes them
weak, numb, and miserable. It seems, in fact,
that there is no greater misfortune than for a
man to feel himself alone in the midst of his
fellow-creatures.

Finally, in " The Gulf," a somewhat imaginary thesis is developed, based on the terrible
vitality which certain vile instincts keep even
in the purest and most innocent minds, while
the story " He Was . . ." shows us the inside
of a clinic, in which there are two dying men
whose illusions of life persist till the supreme
moment.

If we carefully study a few of Andreyev's
characters we can more easily understand his
feelings and his style. Here is, for instance,

Serge Petrovich, a student.   Although he is
not very intelligent, he is above the average.
His mind is preoccupied with all sorts of questions; he reads Nietzsche, he ponders over
many things, but he does not know how to think
for himself.   The fact that there are people
who can find a way to express themselves appears to him as an inaccessible ideal; while
mediocre minds have no attraction for him at
all.   It is from this feeling that all his sufferings come.   So " a horse, carrying a heavy
burden, breathes hard, falls to the ground, but
is forced to rise and proceed by stinging lashes
from a whip."

These lashes are the vision of the superman,
of the one who rightfully possesses strength,
happiness, and liberty.   At times a thick mist
envelops the thoughts of Serge Petrovich, but
the light of the superman dispels this, and he
sees his road before him as if it had been drawn
or told him by another.

Before his eyes there is a being called Serge
Petrovich for whom all that makes existence
happy or bitter, deep and human, remains a
closed book.   Neither religion nor morality,
neither science nor art, exists for him.   Instead of a real and ardent faith, he feels in himself a motley array of feelings.   His habitual
veneration of religious rites mingles with mean
superstitions.   He is not courageous enough to

deny God, not strong enough to believe in Him.
He does not love his fellow-men, and cannot
feel the intense happiness of devoting himself
to his fellow-creatures and even dying for them.
But neither does he experience that hate for
others which gives a man a terrible joy in his
struggle with his fellow-men. Not being capable of elevating himself high enough or falling
low enough to reign over the lives of men, he
lives or rather vegetates with a keen feeling of
his mediocrity, which makes him despair. And
the pitiless words of Zarathustra ring in his
ears: " If your life is not successful, if a venomous worm is gnawing at your heart, know that
death will succeed." And Serge Petrovich,
desperate, commits suicide.

The hero of " At the Window " is quite different. This man has succeeded in building
for himself a sort of fortress, " in which he re-
tires, sheltered from life." Like Serge Petrovich, although not as often, he is tormented by
restless thoughts, and, from time to time, he
is obliged to defend his " fortress." But usually he is contented with watching life, that is
to say, that part which he can see from his window. Nothing troubles the tranquillity of his
mind, not even the desire to live like other men.
One day, he speaks of his theories to a simple,
uneducated young girl whom he thinks of
marrying. She is astonished and stupefied by

them. She perceives that he leads an insipid and morose life. Andrey Nikolayevich does not take into account or understand the stupefaction of the young girl.

" This then is your life? " she asks, incredulously.

" This is it. What more could you want? "

" But it must be terribly monotonous to live in that way, apart from the world."

" What good does one find in mankind? Nothing but tedium. When I am alone, I am my own master, but among men you never know what attitude to take to please them. They drag you into drunkenness, into gambling; then they denounce you to your superiors. I, however, love calmness and frankness. Some of them accept bribes and allow themselves to become corrupt; I do not like that. . . . I adore tranquillity."

Moreover, he does not marry the young girl. He gives her up because he is afraid of the incumbrances that housekeeping will bring.

In " The Grand Slam " four provincial " intellectuals " are locked up in the same fortress, and, by playing cards, they escape the terrible problems of a life which is inimical to them. Their existence has been passed among these cards, which, by a mysterious phenomenon, have become real living creatures to them. One of the players has dreamed all through his life of getting a grand slam, when, one evening, he sees he has the necessary cards in his hand. He has but to take one more card, the ace of spades, and his dream will be realized. But at the very moment when he is stretching forth his hand to take it, he falls down dead. His partners are terrified. One of them, a timorous and exact old man, named Jacob Ivanovich, is particularly struck. A thought comes to him; he quickly rises, after making sure that it was the ace of spades that the dead man was going to take, and cries:

" But he will never know that he was going to get the ace of spades and a grand slam! Never. . . . Never. . . ."

" Then it appeared to Jacob Ivanovich that, up to this moment, he had never understood what death was. Now he understood, and what he saw was senseless, horrible, and irreparable! . . . The dead man would never know! "

The poignant irony of this story is not unusual with Andreyev.

It is again found in the short and symbolic story " The Laugh." A student, profiting by the fact that it is carnival time, disguises himself as a Chinaman and goes to the house of the girl he loves. The mute, immobile, and stupidly calm mask, and the whole " get-up " are so funny, that the unfortunate man rouses irresistible laughter wherever he goes. The young

girl cannot help herself, and, while listening
to his very touching and sincere declaration,
which, at any other time, would have brought
tears to her eyes, she bursts out laughing and
cannot again become serious, although she realizes that a living and unhappy being is hidden
under this impassive and foolish Chinaman's
mask.

In "The Lie" we see a man who, by isola-
ting himself from life, has lost the feeling of
reality, and all capacity of discerning the true
from the false. He suffers terribly from the
feeling that something unknown is happening
around him. This man, who would be ready to
sacrifice everything, even his life, in order to
know truth, guesses the lie that comes between
him and the person who is dearest to him. He
falls into a despair that soon turns to fury.
In order to recover his calm, he begs the girl
he loves, whom he suspects of having deceived
him, to reveal the whole truth to him. But he
cannot believe her protestations of innocence.
One word bursts from his being, breaks forth
from the depths of his soul: "Lies! Lies! Lies
everywhere!"

"In looking at her beautiful pure forehead,"
he writes, "I dreamed that truth was there, on
the other side of that thin barrier, and I felt
a senseless desire to break that barrier and at

least to see the truth. Lower down, beneath
her white breast, I heard the beating of her
heart, and I had a mad desire to open her
breast so that I could read, at least once, what
there was at the bottom of her heart."

He ends by killing that which he loved, and
thinks that he is satisfied: he believes he has
killed the lie.

In " The Thought " we see the gradual development of insanity during the period when
it is doubtful, when the will is almost entirely
annihilated and replaced by a fixed idea, and
when conscience is not entirely abolished. Dr.
Kerzhenzev kills his friend, obeying a mental
suggestion, which now forbids him to do it, now
urges him on. Then, like the " half-insane "
or those sick people who feign madness in order
more easily to attain their end, this man suggests to himself that he is in reality insane.
This idea gets a hold on him after the murder
and fills his soul with mortal terror, the ex-
posure of which forms the most supremely
pathetic part of the whole story. All this
drama of a foundering intelligence, complicated
by bizarre contradictions, is developed with a
penetrating power of analysis.

Andreyev tells us that on the day of judgment the alienists are divided as to the insanity
of Kerzhenzev. The story ends at this place.
But the principal interest of the story does not

lie in this or that solution of the problem, which is not mysterious, for the doctor is doubtlessly abnormal, and it is only as to the degree of insanity that there can be any question. The main interest lies in another direction, in the subtle analysis of this special mental condition, which is done with consummate art.

This story had the honor of occupying an entire meeting of the psychiatrists attached to the Academy of Medicine of St. Petersburg. According to the report of Dr. Ivanov, the assembly was almost unanimous in declaring the murderer insane. Another psychiatrist, who thought he saw proofs of an abnormal mentality in all the stories of Andreyev, pronounced the same verdict against Dr. Kerzhenzev, in a meeting of doctors.

" All of priest Vassily Fiveyisky's life was weighed down by a cruel and enigmatic fatality," — it is thus that the story, " The Life of a Pope," opens. " As if struck by an unknown malediction, he had from his youth been made to carry a heavy burden of sorrows, sickness and misfortunes; he was solitary among men as a planet is among planets; a peculiar and malevolent atmosphere surrounded him. Son of an obscure, patient, and submissive village priest, he also was patient and submissive, and he was a long time in recognizing the particular rancour of destiny. He fell rapidly and arose slowly. Twig by twig he restored his nest. Having become a priest, the husband of a good woman, the father of a son and a daughter, he thought that all was going well with him, that all was solidly established, and that he would remain thus forever. And he blessed God."

But fate was always on the watch for him. It had showed him happiness only to take it away again. After seven years of prosperity, his little son is drowned one summer's day in the river. Death and nameless misfortunes again invade the home of Vassily. One does not live there any more, one prowls around gropingly in a mournful stupor. From morning till evening, his wife comes and goes, silent and indifferent to everything, as if she were looking for some one or something.

In losing his son, poor Vassily has also lost his wife, his helpmate and friend, for the unfortunate woman takes to drink. The faith of the priest holds in this terrible trial. But his misery increases immeasurably. The vice of his wife, his own sick weakness, excite the meanness of the people. Insults have to be borne in silence, tears hidden. At home, the priest's wife has no rest. She has the idea that she can have another son who will take the place of the dead one and be a balm to her broken heart. In her alcoholic desire, a prey to savage fury, she demands that her husband gratify her desire.

" Give him to me, Vassily! Give him back to me, I tell you. . . ."

At last her desire is realized: a son is born to her; but the child, conceived in madness, is born half-witted. The mother takes to drink again, and the despair of Vassily increases. One day the unfortunate woman hangs herself. The pope comes in, however, in time to save her; but now another noose has tightened itself about the priest's heart. One question oppresses him:

" Why these sufferings? If God exists, and if God is love, how is such misery possible? "

Vassily's faith trembles. He decides to leave his cassock, to fly, to put his idiot son out to board and to start life over again. This resolution relieves him. His wife breathes easier. It seems to him that she also can begin a new life. But fate does not loosen its reins.

One day, on coming back from the harvest, he finds his house burned. His wife, in a drunken stupor, had probably set fire to it. She is dying of her burns. Vassily can only sigh. This new misfortune does not put an end to the priest, but rather inspires him. His old faith comes back, he sees in this supreme test a predestination. He kneels down and cries:

" I believe! I believe! I believe! "

From that time on he devotes himself entirely to prayer and macerations. He lives in perpetual ecstasy. The people around him understand nothing of this change and are astounded. Every one of them is waiting for something unusual. And their waiting is not in vain. One day, when he is delivering the funeral oration of a workingman, who has been suddenly killed, Vassily abruptly interrupts the ceremony, approaches the corpse, which has begun to decay, and addresses it thus three times:

" I tell you: arise! "

But the dead man does not move. Then the priest looks at this inert and deformed corpse. He notices the fetid odor that arises from it, the odor of the slow but sure decomposition, and he has a sort of sudden revelation. The scepticism which, for a long time, has been brooding in his heart suddenly is transformed into absolute negation, and addressing himself to Him in whom he had believed, Vassily cries out:

" Thou wishest to deceive me? Then why did I believe? Why hast Thou kept me in servitude, in captivity, all of my life? No free thought! No feeling! No hope! All with Thee! All for Thee! Thee alone! Well, appear! I am waiting! I am waiting! . . . Ah! Thou dost not want to? Very well. . . ."

He does not finish. In a burst of savage

madness he rushes forth from the now empty church. He rushes straight ahead and finally falls in the middle of the road. Death has put an end to his miseries.

" Silence " also shows us a priest, stubborn in his prejudices. This man, Father Ignatius by name, is a sort of rude and authoritative Hercules. All tremble before his stern air, except his daughter, who has decided to continue her studies in St. Petersburg, against the will of her father. Coming back to her home after a long absence, she wanders about, sad and silent. For days at a time she wanders about, pale and melancholy, speaking little, seeking solitude. She hides what oppresses her; she keeps her secret from all. One night, she throws herself under a train, taking her secret with her.

Her grief-stricken mother gets a paralytic stroke which transforms her into a sort of living corpse. The father, crushed by these two catastrophes, which have destroyed all the joy of his life, becomes the prey of a singular mental state: his conscience revolts against the severe maxims and the pitiless prejudices that he has always defended. Tender love, which he has hitherto concealed under his pride, now softens him; he needs affection, and a vague feeling suggests to him that he himself is to blame for all of these misfortunes. His past life, his

daughter, and his wife appear to him as so
many enigmas which raise anguishing questions
in his heart. He calls out, but no one answers.
A death-like silence has invaded the presbytery,
and this silence is especially dreadful near the
paralyzed wife, who is dying without speaking.
Even her eyes do not betray a single thought.
Gradually, a terrible desire to know why his
daughter committed suicide seizes him. At twilight, softly, in his bare feet, he goes up to the
room of his dead daughter and speaks to her.
He entreats her to tell him the truth, to confess to him why she was always so sad, why she
has killed herself. Only the silence answers
him. Then he rushes to the cemetery, where his
daughter's tomb irresistibly attracts him; again
he implores, begs, threatens. For a moment he
thinks that a vague answer arises from the
earth; he places his ear on the rough turf.

"Vera, tell me!" he repeats in a loud and
steady voice.

"And now Father Ignatius feels with terror
that something sepulchrally cold is penetrating
his ear and congealing his brain; it is Vera,
who is continually answering him with the same
prolonged silence. This silence becomes more
and more sinister and restless, and when Father
Ignatius arises with an effort, his face is as
livid as death."

Crushed by the same blind destiny which

annihilated the powerful personality of Father
Ignatius, the piteous and tearful hero of " The
Marseillaise " moves us even more than does the
old priest. The poor fellow cannot grasp the
reason for the ferocity of stupid fate, which
unrelentingly preys upon him. Arrested by
mistake as a revolutionist and condemned to
deportation, he becomes an object of derision
to his comrades. However, gradually, he finds
the strength to share the severe privations of
his companions who have sacrificed themselves
to their ideal of justice and liberty. And, on
his death-bed, he is elated by all that he has
endured; he dreams of liberty, which, up to this
time, had been indifferent to him, and asks
them to sing the Marseillaise over his grave.

" He died, and we sang the Marseillaise. Our
young and powerful voices thundered forth this
majestic song of liberty, accompanied by the
noise of the ocean which carried on the crests
of its waves towards ' dear France,' pale terror and blood-red hope.

" It became our standard forever, the picture
of this nonentity with the hare's body and the
man's heart.

" On your knees to the hero, friends and
comrades!

" We sang. The guns, with their creaking
locks, were pointed menacingly at us; the steel
points of the bayonets were pointed at our

hearts.   The song resounded louder and louder,
with increasing joy.   Held in the friendly hands
of the ' strugglers,' the black coffin slowly sank
into the earth.

" We sang the Marseillaise ! "

The two main characters of " The Gulf," a
student and a school-girl, are walking and discussing rather deep things, such as immortality
and the beauty of pure and noble love.   They
feel some sadness in speaking about these things,
but love appears more and more luminous to
them.   It rises before their eyes, as large as
the world, bursting forth like the sun and mar-
velously beautiful, and they know that there is
nothing so powerful as love.

" You could die for the woman you loved? "
asked Zinochka.

" Of course," replies Nemovetsky unhesi-
tatingly, in a frank and sincere voice, " and
you? "

" I too! "   She remains pensive a moment.
" To die for the one you love, that is a great
happiness!   Would that that were to be my
destiny! "

Gradually night falls.   Nemovetsky and his
companion lose their way in the woods; they
finally arrive in a clearing, where three filthy-
looking men are seated about an empty bottle.
These intoxicated men, whose wicked eyes light

up with a brutal envy of enjoyment and love of destruction, try to quarrel with Nemovetsky, and one of them ends by striking him full in the face with his fist. Zinochka runs away. His heart full of terror, Nemovetsky can hear the shrieks of his friend, whom the vagabonds have caught. Then a feeling of emptiness comes over him, and he loses consciousness. Two of the men throw him into a ravine.

An hour later, Nemovetsky regains consciousness; he gets up with great pain, for he is badly wounded. He remembers what has happened. Fright and despair seize him. He begins to run and call for help with all his strength, at the same time looking among all the bushes, when at his feet, he sees a dim, white form. It is his companion, who lies there motionless. He falls down on his knees and touches her. His hand encounters a nude body, damp and cold, but still living. It seems to grow warm at his touch. He pictures to himself with abominable clearness what the men have done. A feeling of strange strength circulates in his members. On his knees in front of the young girl, in the obscurity of the forest, he tries to bring her back to life, calling her sweet names, caressing her hair, rubbing her cold hands.

" With infinite precautions, but also with deep tenderness, he tries to cover her with the shreds of her torn dress, and the double sensa-

tion of the cloth and the nude body are as keen
as a sword and as inconceivable as madness.
And now he cries for help, now he presses the
sweet and supple body to his breast. His unconscious abandonment unchains the savageness
of his passion. He whispers in a low voice, ' I
love you, I love you.' And throwing himself
violently upon her lips, he feels his teeth entering her flesh.

" Then, in the sadness and impetuousness of
the kiss, the last bit of his mind gives way. It
seems to him that the lips of the young girl
tremble. For an instant, a terrible terror fills
his soul and he sees a horrible gulf yawning at
his feet. . . . And he hurls himself into the
mad throes of his insane passion."

The account of the collegian, which forms
the plot of the story " In the Fog," is even
more daring in its realism. It actually oppresses the reader, not so much by certain details that provoke disgust, as by the analysis
of the sufferings of an unfortunate young man,
whose mind is pure, but who has let himself be
dragged into excesses which are followed by a
sickness of ill name. Severely reprimanded by
his father, the poor young fellow, overcome
with sorrow, the victim of an instinct which he
could not conquer, ends his days in a most horrible way: one evening, he leaves home and goes
out into the streets in an adventuresome spirit.

A half-intoxicated prostitute touches him in passing; he follows her. As they go along, a conversation starts up, and the young man, although she is repugnant to him, goes home with her. Once in her room, a violent quarrel starts up and he kills her, and then commits suicide.

These two stories, especially " The Gulf," caused many lively discussions on the part of the public, and then in the newspapers. Mr. Bourenine, the well-known critic of the " Novoye Vremya," says that he received from several correspondents a series of letters which blamed Andreyev vehemently and requested that this " skunk " of literature be called to order according to his deserts. These protestations were reënforced by an ardent letter from Countess Tolstoy, the wife of the great author, who reproached Andreyev for having so complacently painted such sombre pictures, with such low and violent scenes, all of which tended to pervert youth. The writers were not the only ones to take offence. Two important Russian newspapers organized a sort of inquiry, and they published many of the answers received from the young people of both sexes, but these were all favorable to Andreyev.

In truth, all these judgments are too passionate. It is true that " most of the critics have understood Andreyev only in a superficial manner," as Tolstoy rightfully asserted. The

double impression, for instance, produced by
" The Gulf," is the result of a simple misunder-
standing. Those who think that the adventure
of young Nemovetsky is a slice of life and
characterizes certain psychological states, have,
without a doubt, the right to judge this story
as an indiscretion, and to reproach the author
with a deviation from morality; but Andreyev
has not taken his hero from reality; he has not
tried to give us a picture of manners, but has
expressed an idea, born in his brain under the
influence of the philosophy of Nietzsche. It il-
lustrates the terrible power and the brutality of
a dormant instinct lurking in the purest minds.

Besides, " The Gulf " and " In the Fog " are
compositions which are exceptional in the work
of Andreyev. The idea that he mostly presents
is not the power of bestial instincts, but rather
the indestructible vitality of human feelings and
aspirations towards a better existence, which
sometimes comes to light among the most miserable and depraved people, and even among those
who are in the most abject material condition.
In the destiny of these beings, there are, however, rays of hope. The slightest incident serves
to transform them; suddenly their hearts begin
to beat happily, tears of tenderness moisten
their eyes, they vaguely feel the existence of
something luminous and good. A profound

sensibility, an ardent love of life bursts forth
in their souls. This sensibility, this attachment
to existence, form the theme of four touching
stories: " He Was," " Petka in the Country,"
" The Cellar," and " The Angel."

The action of " He Was " takes place in a
hospital, where a deacon, a foolishly debonair
man, who is attached to his stunted existence,
and a pessimistic merchant, thoroughly satiated,
are at the point of death. The deacon has an
incurable sickness, and his days are numbered.
But he does not know it, and speaks with enthusiasm of the pilgrimage he is going to make
after he is cured, and of the apple-tree in his
garden, which he expects will bear a great deal
of fruit. The fourth Friday of Lent he is taken
into the amphitheatre. He comes back, very
much moved and making the sign of the cross.

" Ah! my brothers," he says, " I am all upset. The doctor made me sit down in a chair
and said to the students: ' Here you see a sick
man.' Ah! how painful it was to hear him add:
' He was a deacon! ' "

" The unfortunate man stopped, and continued in a choking voice: ' " He was a deacon,"
the doctor told them. He told them the story
of my whole life, he even spoke about my wife.
It was terrible! One would have said that I was
dead already, and that he was talking over my
coffin.'

" And as the deacon is thus speaking, all
of the others see clearly that he is going to
die. They see it as clearly as if death itself was standing there, at the foot of the
bed. . . ."

The merchant is a very different sort of man:
he does not believe in God; he has had enough
of life and is not afraid of death. All of his
strength he has spent unnecessarily, without
any appreciable result, without joy. When he
was young he had stolen meat and fruit from
his master. Caught in the act, he had been
beaten, and he detested those who had struck
him. Later on, having become rich, he crushed
the poor with his fortune and scorned those who,
on falling into his hands, answered his hate with
scorn. Finally, old age and sickness had come;
people now began to steal from him, and he, in
turn, beat those whom he caught terribly. And
thus his life had been spent; it had been nothing but a series of transgressions and hatreds,
where the flames of desire, in dying out, had left
nothing but cold ashes in his soul. He refuses
to believe that any one can love this existence,
and he disdainfully looks at the sallow face of
the deacon, and mutters: " Fool! " Then, he
looks at the third man in the room, a young
student who is asleep. This student never fails
to embrace his fiancée, a pretty young girl,
whenever she comes to see him. As he looks the

merchant, more bitterly than before, repeats:
" Fool! "

But death approaches; and this man who
thinks himself superior and who scorns the deacon because he dreams of light and the sun, now
feels disturbed in his turn. In making up the
balance-sheet of this existence which, up to this
time, he believed he hated, he remembers a
stream of warm light which, during the day,
used to come in through the window and gild the
ceiling; and he remembers how the sun used to
shine on the banks of the Volga, near his home.
With a terrible sob, beating his hands on his
breast, he falls back on his bed, right against
the deacon, whom he hears silently weeping.

" And thus they wept together. They wept
for the sun which they were never to see again,
for the apple-tree with fruit which they were not
going to eat, for the shadow that was to en-
velop them, for dear life and cruel death! "

Petka — the hero of " Petka in the Country " — is, at ten years of age, a barber's apprentice. He does not yet smoke as does his
thirteen year old friend Nicolka, whom he wants
to equal in everything. Petka's principal occu-
pation, in the rare moments when the shop is
empty, is to look out of the window at the
poorly dressed men and women who are sitting
on the benches of the boulevard. In the mean-

time, Nicolka goes through the streets of ill
fame, and comes back and tells Petka all his
experiences. The precocious knowledge of
Nicolka astonishes the child, whose one ambition
is to be like his friend one of these days. While
waiting, he dreams of a vague country, but he
cannot guess its location nor its character. And
no one comes to take him there. From morning
till evening he always hears the same jerky cry:
" Some water, boy! "

But one morning his mother, the cook Na-
dezhda, tells the barber that her master and mistress have told her to take Petka to the country
for a few days. Then begins for him an enchanted existence. He goes in bathing four
times a day, fishes, goes on long walks, climbs
trees, rolls in the grass. When, at the end of a
week, the barber claims his apprentice, the child
does not understand: he has completely forgotten the city and the dirty barber-shop; and the
return is very sad. Again is heard the jerky
cry: " Some water, boy! " followed by a menacing murmur of " Come! Come! " if the child
spills any of the water, or has not understood
the orders.

" And, during the night, in the place where
Petka and Nicolka sleep side by side, a weak
little voice speaks of the country, of things that
do not exist, of things that no one has ever
heard of or seen! . . ."

"The Cellar" is inhabited by absolutely
fallen people. A baby has just been born
there. With down-bent necks, their faces unconsciously lighted up by strangely happy
smiles, a prostitute and a miserable drunkard
look at the child. This little life, "weak as a
fire in the steppe," calls to them vaguely, and
it seems to promise them something beautiful,
clear, and immortal. Among the inhabitants of
this cellar, the most unfortunate of all, is a man
named Kizhnakov; he is pale, sickly, worn by
work, almost devoured by suffering and alcohol;
death already lies in wait for him. The most
terrible thing for this man is the necessity of
having to begin to live again each day. He
would like to lie down all day and think of suicide under the heap of rags that serve him as
a covering. He would like best to have some
one come up back of him, and shoot him. He
fears his own voice and his own thoughts. And
it is on him that the baby produces the deepest
impression. Since the birth of the child Kizhnakov does not sleep any more; he tries to protect himself from the cold, and weeps softly,
without sadness and without convulsions, like
those who have pure and innocent hearts, like
children.

"'Why do I weep?' he asks himself.

"Not finding a suitable answer, he replies:
'It is thus. . . .'

" And the meaning of his words is so deep that a new flood of tears come to the eyes of the man whose life is so sad and solitary."

We find the same theme again in " The Angel." A child who also lives in a cellar comes back from a Christmas-tree; he brings with him a toy, and a pretty little wax angel, which he shows to his father. The latter has seen better days, but in the last few years he has been sick with consumption, and now he is awaiting death, silent and continually exasperated by the sight of social injustice. However, the delight of the child infects the father, and both of them have a feeling " of something that joins all hearts into one, and does away with the abyss which separates man from man, and makes him so solitary, unfortunate, and weak." The poor dying man seems to hear a voice from this better world, where he once lived and from which he had been sent forever.

But these are only the dreams of a dying man, the last rays of light of the life which is being extinguished. The ray, penetrating this sick soul, is like the weak sunlight which passes through the dirty windows of a dark hovel.

In his two stories, " The Stranger " and " The Obscure Future," Andreyev shows us two men of entirely different character, animated by generous feelings and a firm will. One of them, a young student, being disgusted with the miseries of Russian life and having decided to expatriate himself, suddenly changes his mind, as a result of the patriotism of one of his friends, a Servian, named Raiko. He makes it his duty never to leave his country, although life there is so terrible and hopeless. There is, in this new feeling, an immense joy and a terrible sadness. The other, the hero of the second story, having one day expressed to his father the hatred he has for the bourgeois life that he is leading, leaves his family, who love him, in order to penetrate the " obscure future."

Evidently, these are people who are fitted to struggle. However, these strugglers, so infrequent in the work of Andreyev, have, in spite of all, something sickly and savage in them; instead of real fighting courage, they possess only extreme audaciousness, mystical rapture, or nervous exaltation. The " obscure future " toward which their eyes are turned is not lighted up by the rays of faith and hope.

The question is whether Andreyev himself believes in the triumph of the elements of life over the elements of death, the horror of which he excels in portraying for us. It is in the following manner that he expresses himself in one of his essays entitled, " Impressions of the Theatre ": " In denying everything, one arrives immediately at symbols. In refuting life, one is but an involuntary apologist. I never believe so much in life as when I am reading the father of pessimism, Schopenhauer! As a result, life is powerful and victorious! . . . It is truth that always triumphs, and not falsehood; it is truth which is at the basis of life, and justifies it. All that persists is useful; the noxious element must disappear sooner or later, will inevitably disappear."

What, then, constitutes the essence of Andreyev's talent is an extreme impressionability, a daring in descriptions of the negative sides of reality, melancholy moods and the torments of existence. As he usually portrays general suffering and sickness rather than definite types, his heroes are mostly incarnations and symbols. The very titles of some of his stories indicate the abstract character of his work. Such are: "Silence," "The Thought," and "The Lie." In this respect he has carried on the work of Poe, whose influence on him is incontestable. These two writers have in common a refined and morbid sensibility, a predilection for the horrible and a passion for the study of the same kind of subjects, — solitude, silence, death. But the powerful fantasy of the American author, which does not come in touch with reality, wanders freely through the whole world and through all the centuries of history. His

heroes take refuge in half-crumbled castles, they
look at the reader from the top of craggy rocks,
whither their love of solitude has led them; even
death itself is not a repulsive skeleton, but
rather a majestic form, full of grandiose mystery.   Andreyev, on the other hand, but rarely
breaks the bounds which unite him to reality.
His heroes are living people, who act, and whose
banal life ends with a banal death.   This realism and this passionate love of truth make the
strength and the beauty of all his work.

A certain harmony between the imaginative
and the real element is characteristic of the best
of Andreyev's productions, especially his last
stories: " The Red Laugh," " The Governor,"
" The Shadows," and " The Seven Who Were
Hanged."

" The Red Laugh " is the symbol, the incarnation, of the bloody and implacable cynicism
of war.   The psychologist of the mysterious
has, in these pages, recorded the terrifying aspects of the Manchurian campaign, which one
could not have foreseen in all of its horror.   He
has shown in a lasting manner the poor human
creature torn from his home, debased to the
rôle of a piece of mechanism.   Not knowing
where he is being led to, he goes, making mur-
derous gestures, the meaning of which he does
not know, without even having the illusory con-

solation of possible personal bravery, being
killed by the shots of an invisible enemy, or,
what is worse, being killed by the shots of his
own comrades — and all of this, automatically,
stupidly. The feeling of terror, the somewhat
mystical intuition of events which, at times,
seem to be paradoxes in the other works of
Andreyev, are perfectly adapted to this terribly real representation of the effects of
war.

The inner drama which Andreyev analyzes in
" The Governor " makes a bold contrast with
the violent pages of " The Red Laugh," the
savage powers of which attain the final limits of
horror.

The governor has during his whole life been
a loyal and strict servant of the Tsar. On the
day of an uprising he mercilessly beat the
enemies of his master ; he blindly accomplished
what he thought was his duty. But, since that
bloody day, a new and unceasing voice speaks
in his conscience. The irreparable act has forever isolated him from his fellow-creatures, and
even from his friends who congratulate him
upon his fine conduct. A stranger to all that is
happening around him, he is left alone to fight
with his conscience, which soon crushes him with
all the weight of remorse. He knows that he
has been condemned by a revolutionary tribunal.
A young girl who is a stranger to him writes

him a compassionate letter: "You are going to be killed," she says, "and that will be justice; but I have great pity for you." This discerning and youthful sympathy penetrates his heart, which finally opens — alas, too late, — to justice and pity.

This marks the beginning of a terrible agony. The governor makes no effort to escape from the fatal judgment. Always alone, he contemplates his terrible distress and awaits the coming of the judiciary. He feels that he has incurred universal blame, and at times he comes to wish for death, which surprises him suddenly as he is turning the corner of a street:

"The whole thing was short and simple, like a scene from a moving-picture play. At a cross-ways, close by a muddy spot, a hesitating voice called to the governor:

"'Your honor!'

"'What?'

"He stopped and turned his head: two men who had come from behind a wall were crossing the street, and were shuffling along in the mud towards him. One of them had in his left hand a piece of folded paper; his other hand was in his pocket.

"And immediately, the governor knew that death had come; and they knew that the governor knew.

"While keeping the paper in his left hand

the unknown man took a revolver out of his
pocket with difficulty.

"The governor glanced about him; he saw
a dirty and deserted square, with bits of grass
growing in the mud, and a wall. But what did
it matter, it was too late! He gave a short but
deep sigh, and stood erect again, fearless, but
without defiance. . . . He fell, with three shots
in his body."

This drama of conscience is set forth with
admirable sureness of analysis, and the author
has been able to represent with impressive intensity the mysterious fatality which demands
the death of the guilty one.

It is this same fatality, under whose hand all
men are equal, which makes the hero of "The
Shadows," a young terrorist who has taken
refuge in a house of ill-fame, obey the strange
desire of his bed-companion.

"Stay with me!" cries the young girl, in
whom is incarnated his destiny, at the moment
that he is going to leave the establishment in
order to escape from the spies who are following him. "You are an honest man! And I've
been waiting five years to meet an honest man.
. . . Stay with me, because you belong to me."

After a terrible internal combat the man
yields to this unknown will which is oppressing
him. A traitor to his party, he decides to be-

come the companion of this painted girl, with
whom he then gets drunk.

" As long as I am in the shadows," he murmurs with the sombre resignation of an Andreyev hero, " I might as well remain there."

At dawn, the police come to arrest him. And
while his friend tries desperately to resist the
agents of the force, he contemplates the brutal
scene with an ironic smile.

" The Seven Who Were Hanged," written in
1908, right after the executions at Kherson
and Warsaw, shows us pictures of terror and
fright aptly described by the genius of Andreyev. This work has prodigious color and
strength, and one experiences deep emotions on
reading it. Five terrorists, captured at the
very moment when they are going to assassin-
ate a minister, and two criminals, are condemned to be hanged on the same day. The
writer shows them to us tortured by the most
horrible anguish, that which immediately pre-
cedes death. The word " madness " appears on
every page: mystical madness of hallucination
that hears music and voices, such is that of the
young revolutionary Moussya; then there is
the brutal madness of her comrades Kashirine
and Golovine, who are ready to scream with
terror; the madness of the victims, the frenzy
of the executioners.

The night before the execution the prisoners
are visited by their relatives. The farewell
which Serge Golovine takes of his family is
rightly considered one of the most poignant
and most cleverly constructed scenes that Andreyev has ever written.

Followed by his mother, who totters along,
Serge's father, a retired colonel, enters the
room where visitors are received. Serge does
not know that the colonel spent the whole night
in preparing for this meeting. He has told
his wife what to do: embrace her son, keep
from crying, and say nothing. But the unhappy mother in the presence of her son cannot control her emotions; her eyes are strained
and she breathes faster and faster.

" Don't torture him! " commands the colonel.

Several stupid and insignificant words are
exchanged in order to hide the terrible suffering
that they all are going through. The visit
ends: the parents must bid their son good-bye
forever. The mother gives her son a short kiss,
then she shakes her head and murmurs, trembling:

" ' No, it is not that! It is not that! '

" ' Good-bye, Serge,' says his father.

" They shake hands, and give each other a
brief but hearty kiss.

" ' You . . .'" begins Serge.

" ' What's that? ' asks his father in a jerky voice.

" ' No, not like that. No, no! What was I going to say? ' repeats his mother, shaking her head.

" She was again seated, trembling.

" ' You . . .' continues Serge.

" Suddenly, his face took on a pitiful expression, and he made a grimace like a child. The tears then came to his eyes.

" ' Father, you are a strong man! '

" ' What are you saying? What are you saying? ' the colonel cries, frightened.

" Then, as if he had been struck, the colonel's head sank down upon his son's shoulder. And they kissed each other, again and again, the one with white hair and the other with the prisoner's ' capote.'

" ' And I? ' a hoarse voice brusquely asked.

" They looked: the mother was standing, her head thrown back, and she was watching them with anger, almost hate.

" ' What is the matter, dear? ' cried the colonel.

" ' And I? ' she repeated. ' You two kiss each other, and I? You are men, aren't you? And I? '

" ' Mother! '

" And Serge threw himself into his mother's arms. . . .

" The last words of the colonel were:

" ' I consecrate you to death, my boy! Die with courage, like a soldier! ' "

These few lines retrace one of the thousands of daily dramas which compose modern Russian history. The work of Andreyev brings to us a sad vibrant echo of the sobs which ring out in Russian dungeons. And this faithful portrayal of events, events so frequent that they no longer move us from our indifference, when we find the echo of them in the press, will raise in the conscience of Andreyev's readers a cry of horror and pity.

It is principally in the dramas which he has written in the last few years [11] that Andreyev has developed with most force and clearness his favorite themes: the fear of living and dying, the madness of believing in free-will, and the nonsense of life, the weakness and vanity of which he depicts for us.

The first of these works to appear was " The Life of Man," which is a tragic illustration of this pessimism.

When the curtain rises, " some one in grey," holding a torch, informs the audience that Man is about to be born. From this time on, his life, lighted like a lamp, will burn until death extinguishes it. And Man will live, docile and obedient to the orders that come to him from

On-High, through the intermediary of this
" some one," whom he does not know. Each
act of the play represents a period in the life
of Man. In the first act, Man has acquired
riches and glory, and is found feasting with his
friends in his sumptuous home. The guests
are enchanted with their host, whom they envy.
But happiness is a fugitive shadow; it soon
betrays the man, who becomes poor, loses his
son, falls into the most abject misery, and dies
in a filthy and infected cellar, surrounded by
vile beggars, while the torch, held by " some
one in grey," begins to grow weaker, and then
dies out. And the man, conscious of his power-
lessness to conquer fate, and conscious of his
weakness in face of the mysterious " some one
in grey," confounds in the same malediction
God, Satan, Fatality, and Life, who have united
to annihilate him.

The themes of the " King of Famine " and
" Black Masks " offer a certain analogy to the
theme of " The Life of Man."

From the top of a belfry the " King of
Famine," in company with " Time " and
" Death," incites a workingmen's revolt. He
inspires them with an absolute certainty of victory, although he can see that the revolt will
be quelled and the rebels crushed. Events do
not delay, in fact, to verify the prophecy of
the monarch. Locked up, the leaders of the

revolt are condemned to death. The scene of
judgment in the last act is one of the finest in
the play. On one side are seated the sad and
dull judges; on the other, the elegant public,
which, with a feeling of fear and disgust, gazes
at the unfortunates whom the King of Famine
has robbed of almost all human semblance.
And in this play, also, Death reaps a bountiful
harvest.

" Black Masks " is the study of a pathological case which Andreyev has dramatized
after the fashion of de Maupassant's " The
Horla."

The Duke Lorenzo, young, noble, and the
owner of a magnificent palace, is getting ready
to receive his guests, to whom he is giving, on
this evening, a masked ball. The masks arrive;
they are all black, and all look alike. They all
crowd around Lorenzo, whom this funereal sort
of masquerade bothers extremely. He cannot
find his wife among the guests. In fact, he
does not recognize any of them until, to cap
the climax, he meets his double, fights with him
and dies, without being able to discern who is
the real Lorenzo.

At times, Andreyev tries to find the justification of life, and looks for it in mysticism. He
then expounds a doctrine, according to which,
truth is individual and perhaps conceived by

each man, thanks to direct intuition. Such is
the mystical truth which the author tries to
affirm in " Anathema."

The play opens with a scene between Anathema, the incarnation of Satan, and " He who
guards the gates," behind which is the mystery
of eternity. Anathema entreats the Guardian
to . give him access. But it is in vain that
Anathema flatters and insults him; finally,
Anathema declares that he will choose from
among mankind a poor Jew, named David
Leiser, will enrich him and, in order to prove
the absolute nonsense of life, will make this man
a living protestation against the work of Him
who knows all. Disguised as the lawyer Nullius,
Anathema comes down to earth and gives millions to David. The latter, the best of men,
distributes his riches among the poor. But the
beggars become more and more numerous, and
soon David finds that he is as poor as he was
before the visit of Anathema.

In the meantime, the crowd of paupers, always increasing, ask more money from David;
they demand miracles from this man, whose
goodness has made him a saint, a superman, in
their eyes. They bring him corpses and ask
him to resuscitate them. David flees; the
crowd follows and stones him to death. But,
through his love for his fellow-men, David has
acquired immortality, as " He who guards the

gates " tells Anathema, when, in the last act, the
evil archangel, beaten, returns to lie on the
threshold of the inconceivable mysterious.

This admirable play, born of a philosophical
conception which relates it to Goethe's
" Faust," has been received with particular
interest. Andreyev, in writing it, has come
very near to solving the question of the meaning of life, and its justification. And, to the
person who ponders a while over this work, it
will appear that it is not Anathema who entreats " Him who guards the gates " to reveal
the mystery, but it is Andreyev himself, who,
carried away by the force of his genius, has
thrown himself, as if at an invincible wall,
against this pitiless guardian, the guardian of
the solution of the enigma of life.

While " Anathema " is an abstract character, whose form resembles more an algebraic
formula than a living process of human relations, another of Andreyev's plays, " The Love
of the Student," written a short time before
" Anathema," gives us a little picture of customs, alert and painted with the touch of a
master.

Gloukortzev, a young student, falls in love
with a young girl whom her mother forces to
become a prostitute. Gloukortzev, young and
inexperienced, has not the slightest suspicion,
till the young girl herself reveals to him the

horrible truth. And, perhaps for the first time in his life, the gulf of necessity, toward which fate drives men, opens before him. He sees with horror that he cannot come to the rescue of the girl he loves, because he is poor himself. He cannot even buy her some food, when she tells him that she has eaten nothing since the night before. Placed before the absolute bare reality of life, Gloukortzev does not know what to do, and his comrades, good and upright fellows like himself, have not the means to help him.

Several very successful scenes, in which the author blends the tragic with the comic, deserve, in this brief analysis, special attention. In the first act, there is a students' picnic at which Olga and Gloukortzev, still full of happiness, are present. The spectator is drawn by personal sympathy to the student Onoufry, a good fellow, always drunk, who makes fun of others and himself. We see him again in the second act, when Gloukortzev finds out about Olga's life. The poignant scene between the poor girl and her lover is heightened and softened by the arrival of the students, to whom Gloukortzev tells his sorrow. The last two acts take place in Olga's home. The mother brings her daughter a rich " client." And, in the next room, Gloukortzev suffers terribly, because he knows that his beloved is still leading an infamous life. In the same room, in the fourth act, we are present at an orgy, during which the student quarrels with an officer who has come to spend the night with Olga. But Onoufry, interfering in time, prevents an affray the issue of which would probably have been fatal. When the curtain falls, Gloukortzev, intoxicated, is weeping; at his side is Olga, also weeping, while Onoufry and the officer are singing: "The days of our lives are as short as the life of a wave."

This drama, as well as most of Andreyev's plays, has been produced with great success in Russia and also in Europe.

VII

DMITRY MEREZHKOVSKY

UNLIKE Gorky, Andreyev, and Tchekoff, Merezhkovsky was brought up in the midst of comfort and elegance; he received a correct and careful education; fate was solicitous for him, in that it allowed him to develop that spirit of objective observation and calm meditation which permits a man to look down on the spectacle of life, and indulge in philosophical speculations very often divorced from reality.

The son of an official of the imperial court, Merezhkovsky was born in St. Petersburg in 1865. In this city he received his entire education, and here he gained the degree of bachelor of letters in 1886.

He began his literary career with some poems which won for him a certain renown. In 1888, he published his first collection, and then a second in 1892, " The Symbols." At the same time, he published several translations from Greek and Latin authors.

As he was a friend of the unfortunate Nadson, and a pupil of the humanitarian Pleshcheyev, Merezhkovsky wrote at first under the influence of the liberal ideas of his early masters. His verses, always harmonious, and a little affected, soon belied this tendency and very frankly revealed his preferences. In the first collection of his poems, vibrant with generous ideas, he proclaimed that he wanted, above all, " the joy of life," and that a poet should not have any other cult than that of beauty.

The poem called " Vera " was his first real success. The extreme simplicity of the plot — the unfortunate love of a young professor and of a young weakly girl who dies of consumption in the very flower of youth — and the very faithful reproduction of the intellectual life of Russia in 1880, give to this work the importance of a document in some ways almost historic.

This poem is like a last tribute paid by the author to the humanitarian and realistic tendencies of Russian literature. Afterward, yielding to the inclinations of his nature and his taste for classical antiquity, Merezhkovsky insensibly changed. While acquiring, both in prose and in verse, an incontestable mastery, he could now look only for a cold and haughty beauty which was sufficient unto itself. The beginning was hard, but then all came easier. After critical articles on the trend of modern literature, he published " The Reprobate," a bold dithyrambic on ancient Greek philosophy. The poetry that followed was clearly Epicurean and in complete contradiction to the altruistic tendencies of the neo-Christian period, which found an arch enemy in Nietzsche, whose philosophy evidently influenced Merezhkovsky. However, this evolution did not have a very favorable effect on his poetry; it bordered on an art the clarity of which approached dryness, while at the same time its lack of tenderness reduced its symbolism to an artificial lyricism or to lifeless allegories.

Merezhkovsky works with untiring constancy to glorify antiquity. He has made excellent translations of Sophocles, Euripides, and of " Daphne and Chloe," that idyl of Longus that charmed both Goethe and Catherine II. He chooses the characters of his new poems from Greek and Latin mythology, and from themes inspired by an ardent love of paganism. He has written three prose works of considerable value: " The Death of the Gods," " The Resurrection of the Gods," [12] and " Peter and Alexis." The general idea of all of these is the struggle between Greek polytheism and Christianity, between Christ and Antichrist, to use the author's expression, or, as Dostoyevsky used to say, between the " man-God " and the " God-man."

This struggle touches upon the gravest problem that can occupy the human mind, and continually puts before us this perplexing question: " Should the purpose of life be only the search for happiness and beauty, or must we admit, as a law of nature, the dogma of suffering and death? " The former of these conceptions found its supreme formula in Greek paganism. The ultimate expansion of the latter leads us, on the one hand, to faith, — to the religion of sacrifice, and, on the other hand, into the domain of philosophy, — to the destruction of the desire to live, as conceived by Schopenhauer. It is this struggle between the two principles of Hellenic philosophy and Christian faith that Merezhkovsky has tried to show us by fixing, in his novels, the historic moments when this struggle reached its greatest intensity; and by making appear in these periods the characters who, according to him, are most typical and representative. For this reason he has chosen to give his readers pictures of the three epochs which he considers as culminating: first, the last attempt made to restore the worship of the gods a short time after the Emperor Constantine had brought about their ruin; secondly, the Renaissance, which, in spite of triumphant Christianity, shows us a glorious renewal of the arts and sciences of antiquity; finally, the beginning of the 18th century, the reign of Peter the Great, who tried to make a place for the gods of antiquity in Russia, where they were regarded with horror by the orthodox clergy.

In his novel, " The Death of the Gods," Merezhkovsky has painted the first of these epochs, the different phases of which revolve about the principal hero, the emperor Julian the Apostate. In " The Resurrection of the Gods " he develops, in sumptuous frescoes, the age of the Renaissance, personified by Leonardo da Vinci, who best typifies the character and tendencies of that time. In " Peter and Alexis," he retraces Russian life in the beginning of the 18th century, when it was dominated by the extraordinary character of Peter the Great.

Julian the Apostate was one of the last idolaters of expiring paganism. But he could do nothing against the infatuation of the masses who were embracing the new religion, and it was in vain that he employed both so much kindness and so much violence in order to suppress Christianity. The reign of the gods was irrevocably ended. His soul filled with rage when he saw that he was powerless to change the course of events. He ended by undertaking a foolhardy expedition into Persia, thinking that that was the only way in which to defeat Christ, triumph

over the "cursed" religion, and bring back
victoriously the altars of the dead gods. But
the Olympians on whom he had counted were of
no service to him. According to the Christian
legend, it was then, at the moment of death, that
he cried out: "Galilean, thou hast conquered!"
They say that he added: "Let the Galileans
conquer, for the victory will be ours, . . . later.
The gods will come back . . . we shall all be
gods."

This scene is one of the finest in the book.
Surrounded by some faithful friends, Julian
speaks, with his last breath, the words which
one of these friends, the historian Ammianus
Marcellinus, has recorded.

"His voice was low but clear. His whole
presence breathed forth intellectual triumph,
and from his eyes there still gleamed invincible
will. Ammianus's hand trembled as he wrote.
But he knew that he was writing on the tables
of history, and transmitting to future generations the words of a great emperor:

"'Listen, friends; my hour is come, perhaps too soon. But you see that I, like an
honest debtor, rejoice in giving back my life
to Nature, and feel in my soul neither pain nor
fear; nothing but cheerfulness, and a presentiment of eternal repose. . . . I have done my
duty, and have nothing to repent. From the
days when, like a hunted animal, I awaited

death in the palace of Marcellum, in Cappa-
docia, up to the time when I assumed the purple
of the Roman Cæsars, I have tried to keep my
soul spotless. If I have failed to do all that I
desired, do not forget that our earthly deeds
are in the hands of Fate. And now I thank the
Eternal Ruler for having allowed me to die,
not after a long sickness nor at the hands of
an executioner, but on the battlefield, in full
youth, with work ahead of me still to be done.
. . . And, my dear friends, tell both my friends
and my enemies, how the Hellenes, endowed with
divine wisdom, can die. . . .' "

Revenge for the dying emperor was long in
coming. But now, after eleven centuries, the
prophecy of Julian is accomplished: heroic antiquity, everlastingly young, arises from the
grave. On all sides the gods are resurrected.
Their marble effigies, so long buried, reappear.
Both the powerful and the humble receive them
with enthusiasm and rejoice at seeing them. It
is an irresistible outburst which carries with it
all classes of the Italian people. Like a wind-
blown flame, Greek genius inspires a new life
in the world. But, while a sweeter and more
humane moral feeling tries to liberalize the
church, the sombre voice of Savonarola, hard-
ened by the terrible corruption of manners,
mounts ever more menacingly:

" Oh, Italy! oh, Rome! I am going to deliver you up into the hands of a people who will efface you from among the nations. I see them, the enemies who descend like hungry tigers. . . . Florence, what have you done? Do you want me to tell you? Your iniquity has heaped up the measure; prepare for a terrible plague! Oh, Lord, thou art witness that I tried to keep off this crumbling ruin from my brothers; but I can do no more, my strength is failing me. Do not sleep, oh, Lord! Dost Thou not see that we are becoming a shame to the world? How many times we have called to Thee! How many tears we have shed! Where is Thy providence? Where is Thy goodness? Where is Thy fidelity? Stretch forth Thy helping hand to us! "

And thus the antagonism between the " Godman " and the " man-God " of Hellenic paganism expresses itself more strongly than ever before.

The picture of the Renaissance that Merezhkovsky paints for us is very full, very rich, at times even a little overburdened with episodes and people. One constantly rubs shoulders with Leonardo da Vinci, the duchess Beatrice of Este, regent of Milan, the favorite Lucrecia Crivelli, the mysterious Gioconda, Charles VIII, Louis XII and Francis I, kings of France, and also with Cæsar Borgia; we find here the preaching of Savonarola, the death of the pope

Alexander VI (Borgia), Marshal Trivulce, the
triumphal entry of the French into Milan, the
diplomacy of Niccolo and Machiavelli.   In
fact, as has been said above, there are too many
events and characters.

Two centuries go by and now we come to the
third novel, " Peter and Alexis."   The scene is
in Russia, and the hero is Peter the Great, whom
Merezhkovsky represents as a worshipper of
things Olympian.   He gives a magnificent description of the orgies held by the emperor in
honor of Bacchus and Venus, especially the
latter, whose statue he expressly ordered from
Rome and installed in the Summer Garden at
St. Petersburg.

In a veritable fairyland of avenues, of yoke-
elms and flower-beds in geometric designs, of
enormous baskets filled with the choicest flowers,
of straight canals, of ponds, of islets, of magnificent fountains, such a fairyland as Watteau
would have dreamed of, there is a Venetian
fête with all sorts of fire-works and illumina-
tions ; small crafts, adorned with flags, are filled
with men in golden garments, girded with
swords, and wearing three-cornered hats and
buckled shoes ; and the women are dressed in
velvet and covered with jewels.

The Tsar himself opens the case, and helps in
placing the goddess on her pedestal.   Again,

as two hundred years before in Florence, the resurrected goddess, Aphrodite, emerges from the grave. The cords stretch, the pulleys creak; she rises higher and higher. Peter is almost of the same superhuman height as the statue. And his face, close to that of Aphrodite, remains noble: the man is worthy of the goddess. . . .

" The Immortal One — Aphrodite — was still the same that she was on the hillside in Florence; she had progressed further and further, from age to age, from people to people, halting nowhere, till in her victorious march she had reached the very ends of the earth, the Hyperborean Scythia, beyond which there is naught but darkness and death. . . ."

But what miseries this magnificent façade conceals! Not far off, on an island in the river, one can see people who are watching the fête and who think that they are present at one of the spectacles forerunning doomsday. Among the crowd are seen the " raskolnik " Cornelius, old Vitalya of the " runners," deserters, the merchant Ivanov, the clerk Dokounine . . . and several others. In the few remarks that they exchange, we can see that, for them, Peter the Great is the Antichrist, " the beast announced by the Gospel."

Such is the tie that binds Peter the Great, Julian, and Leonardo together. But this tie is weakened by the fact that Peter, an essentially practical and utilitarian genius, was not the man to become inspired with Hellenic poetry, and if the author introduces the Tsar into the society of Julian the Apostate and of Leonardo da Vinci, it is because Peter the Great was one of those indefatigable strugglers, who, to attain their ends, put themselves above the obligations of ordinary morality, one of those supermen, who hesitate at nothing in satisfying the instincts of their egoisms, of their dominating wills.   In fact, the heroes of Merezhkovsky's novels all belong in the category of the Nietzschean type of superman, which explains their philosophical relationship and the sort of trilogy which these three novels form.   Thus, Julian the Apostate, who tried in vain during his life to make history repeat itself, by transplanting pagan traditions into a plot which had become unfit to receive them, and who died in the effort to preserve a faith — does not this man, then, incarnate that implacable pursuit of the " integral personality " so extolled by Nietzsche?   Leonardo da Vinci, that great universal and keen mind, who gave himself over to all the impulses of his creative genius, not caring whether the impulses are worthy or harmful, appears as a luminous manifestation of that state of the soul " beyond good and bad " which characterizes the superman.   And

is not Peter the Great also a veritable superman;
a man who, through his iron will, upset all the
ancient institutions of aged Russia, and who
did not even prevent the assassination of his
son Alexis, inasmuch as he thought that it was
for the good of his country?

At all events, the interest and value of " Peter
and Alexis " does not rest in its philosophic
ideas and in the Nietzschean obsession, but
rather in the art with which Merezhkovsky
faithfully depicts the psychology of his heroes.
The successive phases of this terrible tragedy
lead up to a striking climax, and set off, one
against the other, temperaments so entirely opposed that the reciprocal tenderness of the
father and son is transformed finally into suspicion and hate, and the father resolves to sacrifice the life of his son to what appears to him
to be the right of the State. The novel, although a little overburdened with details, is an
excellent analysis of the customs of the Russia
of former times.

The source of the struggle between Peter
and Alexis was known. Peter represented the
West and the new ideas, while Alexis represented
the Russia of old, rebellious to innovations
which she considered dangerous. The author
thus symbolizes the eternal conflict between the
past and the future. He has analyzed with
consummate art the characters of his two heroes.

Peter is a man full of contrasts; he is, like many Russians, " a brute and a child," by turns violent and gentle, knavish and simple, cruel and kind, practical and mystical, proud and modest. Possessed of a prodigious activity, he conceives tremendous projects which he immediately wants to put into execution, inspecting everything, verifying everything, finding no care beneath his dignity, talking to the workingmen as if he were one of them, not making long speeches, and fiercely, with cries of rage, fighting dishonest contractors and tradesmen.

'Set over against this irascible father, endowed with herculean strength, the Tsarevich Alexis, thin, pale, and delicate, makes a sad figure. Most historians, following the example of Voltaire, have represented this prince as a narrow-minded person, a victim of the bigoted and intolerant education of the clergy. Merezhkovsky, a more discreet psychologist, does not rely on these superficial data, but shades the portrait admirably. He makes Alexis an intelligent man, not like his father, but a man with a comprehensive, subtle spirit. He probably was crushed by the powerful individuality of his father. As he is closely in touch with the people, and knows their aspirations, Alexis judges the work of his father with delicate insight: " My father hopes," he says,

" to do everything in a great hurry. One, two, three, and the affair is settled. He does not realize that things done hastily do not last. . . ."

While Peter is aware of his unpopularity, his son is loved by the townspeople, the peasants, and the clergy. They say that, " Alexis is a man who seeks God and who does not want to upset everything: he is the hope of the nation."

What the author has best shown in this novel is the degree to which the high society of this time was, under its exterior gorgeousness, barbarous and vulgar. A German girl, maid-of-honor to the wife of Alexis, defines it in the following way: " Brandy, blood, coarseness. It is hard to say which is most prominent, — perhaps it is coarseness." The boyards [13] she describes as: " Impudent savages, baptized bears, who only make themselves more ridiculous when they try to ape the Europeans."

As is evident, these three works of Merezhkovsky belong to the " genre " of the historical and philosophical novel which demands, besides the power to call up past ages, a careful education and the gift of clear-sightedness. And the novelist completely fulfills these requirements. He knows his subject, he studies all the necessary documents with the greatest care and follows every story to its source; finally, before taking up his pen, he visits the countries and the cities in which the stories take place. Thus, in order better to understand Leonardo da Vinci, in order to live his life, the author of "The Resurrection of the Gods" traversed Italy and France from one end to the other, in the same way that he had traveled all over Greece so that he could give us a more life-like Julian. With the same care, he spent a long time reading Russian historical documents in order to present the reader with a better picture of the customs of the time of Peter the Great. The result is a series of historical pictures, almost perfect in their accuracy. If Merezhkovsky had no other merit than this faithful portrayal of the past, his novels even then would be read with interest and pleasure.

Some critics have remarked that the most glaring defect in his books lies in their construction. His novels often disregard the laws relating to this sort of literature, which demand the clever grouping of the characters and events around a principal hero. It is true that this unity and the sense of proportion absolutely necessary for any sort of harmony are not to be found in his works. The details predominate to the detriment of important facts; the people of secondary importance are sometimes drawn better than the heroes themselves, whose ad-

ventures are entirely unconnected. There is a
series of jumps from one situation to another,
with gaps and interruptions of considerable
length, which break the chain of events. It is
for this reason that, instead of seeing a historical fresco, we see a whole gallery of sketches,
executed with subtle artistry, but insufficiently
connected with the main action of the drama.

These observations apply especially to the
first attempt of the young author: " The Death
of the Gods "; " The Resurrection of the
Gods " and " Peter and Alexis " are more skil-
fully composed. They indicate a stronger
tendency towards unity; one feels that an in-
finitely firmer and more experienced brush has
been used; the colors are richer and they do
not suffer from that monotony of effect and
of color so noticeable in " The Death of the
Gods," where the author too often uses the same
devices. As to the characters of Leonardo da
Vinci and Peter the Great, they are very carefully worked out, and the events in the lives
of the Italian master and the Russian Tsar are
narrated with magnificent psychological analysis, which forces the reader to sympathize with
the heroes even more than he would naturally.

Merezhkovsky has also been accused of being
over-educated. The innumerable documents
presented do not bear closely enough upon the
action, the result being that many of his pages

read like mere annals. They interest the reader
but do not move him. This is one reason why
some critics, essentially different in spirit from
Merezhkovsky, have believed themselves right
in denying that he has any talent. But this
accusation falls of itself in the face of the
power of the inspiration which pervades his
work, and the dramatic sense which he displays
in setting forth the events and personages. It
is impossible, for instance, to read without the
deepest emotion the story of the last days of
Leonardo da Vinci, where the author establishes
the tragic contrast between the outward signs
of glory, the superficial honors with which this
genius is overwhelmed, and the moral solitude
which afflicts him to the very end, which comes
when he is among people who are strangers to
his soul. All the childhood recollections of this
same Da Vinci are full of charm. There is a
veritable master spirit shown in the chapters
in which the author portrays for us the enigmatic and seductive Mona Lisa. Finally, he
has given us a relief of rare energy in the terrible struggle between Peter and Alexis, between the man of iron whom nothing can affect
and his son, kind and timid, who, while having
a mortal fear of his father, still loves him. As
to certain pages, like those which describe the
strange inner life of the Tsarina Marfa Mat-
veyevna, " living by the light of candles, in an

old house savouring of the oil of night-lamps, the dust and the putrification of centuries," these pages are a veritable tour de force if only because of the plasticity and richness of the author's vocabulary.

Finally, what tragic horror there is in the supreme struggle where the emperor, the assassin of his son, sees his isolation and feels his weakness, " like a large deer gnawed at by flies and lice until the blood runs! "

Besides his novels Merezhkovsky has published several essays, on Pushkin, Maykov, Korolenko, Calderon, the French neo-romanticists, Ibsen and others. . . . The most important of all are: " The Causes of the Decadence of Modern Russian Literature " and " Tolstoy and Dostoyevsky." He reveals here a fine and penetrating power of observation, which, however, is often obscured because of his obsession by Nietzschean ideas. Moreover, he does not hide his antipathy to the people whose literary tastes and ideas differ from his. From this characteristic comes strange exaggerations and a somewhat limited appreciation of men and events. An example of this, for instance, is the impression that he gives in his study of the causes of the decadence of modern Russian literature, the subject of which imposes upon the author the double task of look-

ing up the causes of this decadence and also
proving that it exists. He has not succeeded.
In fact, it appears that this idea of decadence
exists only in the minds of the author and of a
small circle of writers who have the same ideas
about the mission of literature. Merezhkovsky
is absolutely right in all that he says about the
fact that Russian writers live solitary, deprived
of that precious excitation which is felt when
one is in contact with original and different
temperaments; but if you add to this, as he
has done, the statement that Russia does not
possess a literature worthy of the name, you
go too far. Without being a great scholar, it
is easy to perceive that our contemporary Russian authors are legitimate sons of Turgenev,
Dostoyevsky and Tolstoy, and grandsons of
Gogol, who himself is closely related to Pushkin. A democratic and humanitarian realism
— widely separated from the Nietzscheism of
Merezhkovsky — strongly characterizes the
Russian lineage.

In his book on Tolstoy and Dostoyevsky he
spends a long time in differentiating between
the artistic intuition of these two great masters,
who are, according to him, the most profound
expression of the popular and higher element
of Russian culture.

What strikes him first in Tolstoy is the insistence with which he describes " animal man."

In a kind of " leitmotiv " Merezhkovsky has shown us the Tolstoyan characters individualized by very particular corporal signs. " Tolstoy," he says, " has, to the very highest degree, the gift of clairvoyance of the flesh; even when dead, the flesh has a tongue." He is the subtle painter of all sensations and he is a master in this domain. But his art diminishes singularly, and even disappears when he tries to analyze the soul within the flesh. Dostoyevsky, on the other hand, triumphs in his dialogue; one sees his characters because one shares all their sadness, their passions, their intelligence, and their sensibility. Dostoyevsky is the painter of the depths of the human soul, which he portrays with almost supernatural acuteness. And, as Tolstoy is " the seer of the flesh," so is Dostoyevsky " the seer of the soul."

Having established this difference in principle, Merezhkovsky, by constant deduction, concludes, in consonance with his favorite idea, that Tolstoy personifies " the pagan spirit " at its height, while Dostoyevsky represents " the Christian spirit." There is a great deal of fine drawn reasoning in all of this, some very original ideas, but a great many paradoxes. Even the very personality of Tolstoy, the analysis of which occupies a large part of the book, is belittled in the hands of Merezhkovsky. Instead of a noble character, one sees a very vain person, preoccupied only with himself. It is in this simple way that Merezhkovsky explains the moral evolution which led Tolstoy to make those long and sad studies of a kind of life compatible with the true good of humanity, and forced him to them by " the anguish of the black mystery of death " which, having got possession of the author of " Anna Karenin " in his sixtieth year, in the midst of a life of prosperity, made him hate his fortune and his comfort, which formerly had been so dear to him. In the refusal of Tolstoy to "bow to the great authorities of the literary world, such as Æschylus, Dante, and Shakespeare," a refusal which is only the logical consequence of his ideas on the principle and purpose of art, Merezhkovsky can only see a lack of general culture. Finally, the sort of life he led toward the end of his days came only " from the desire to know and taste the pleasure of simplicity in all its subtleties." " The admirable Epicurus," says Merezhkovsky, " that joyous sage, who, in the very center of Athens, cultivated with his own hands a tiny garden, and taught men not to believe in any human or divine chimeras, but to be contented with the simple happiness that can be given by a single sunbeam, a flower, a sup of water from an earthen cup, or the summer time, would recognize in Tolstoy his faithful disciple, the only one, perhaps, who survives in this barbaric silence, where American comfort, a mixture of effeminacy and indigence, has made one forget the real purpose of life. . . ."

In writing these lines, Merezhkovsky must have forgotten that Tolstoy, in proclaiming his ideas on religion and humanity, prepared himself, not for Epicurean pleasures, but for seclusion in one of the terrible dungeons of a Russian monastery (now in disuse) under the persecutions of a temporal and secular authority, and it was not his fault that, by a sort of miracle, he escaped this fate.

Dostoyevsky's life is the exact opposite of Tolstoy's. The story of Dostoyevsky's terrible existence is probably known. Born in an almshouse, he never ceased to suffer, and to love. . . . It is hard to think of two people more absolutely different than Tolstoy and Dostoyevsky. But Merezhkovsky loves violent contrasts; in the sharp difference between these two writers, he sees the permanent union of two controlling ideas of the Russian Renaissance and the imminence of a final sympathy, symbolic of a concluding harmony.

We have, by turns, studied Merezhkovsky as a poet, a novelist, and a critic. The greatest merit of his literary personality rests in the perfect art with which he calls up the past. But Merezhkovsky is not only an artist. As we have noted, his novels have, as their end, one of the greatest contradictions of human life, — the synthesis of the voluptuous representations of the religion of classical antiquity and the moral principles of Christianity. It is, therefore, natural to ask whether he has in any way approached his goal and just where he sees the salvation of humanity, the present situation of which seems to him desperate. The answer to this question can be found in his book, " Ham Triumphant." [14] Our study of Merezhkovsky's literary character would be incomplete if the ideas of this book were not set forth.

According to Merezhkovsky, the present evil in the world consists entirely in the moral void which results from the disappearance of the Christian ideal from the soul. The loss of this ideal was inevitable, and even productive of good, because it had been so mutilated and deformed by the Church, that Christian religion became a symbol of the reaction, and its God synonymous with executioner. Humanity will rid itself of Christianity. But nothing will replace it, unless it be the philosophy of positivism, a sort of material religion of the appetites and the senses, which gives no answer to our anguish and our mystical instincts. This philosophy presided at the formation of a miserable society, an egotistical and mediocre bourgeoisie, who have no spiritual tendencies, and are incapable of sacrificing themselves to any ideal other than that of money.

John Stuart Mill said that the bourgeoisie would transform Europe into a China; the Russian publicist Hertzen, frightened by the victories of socialism, in 1848, foresaw the end of European civilization, drowned in a wave of blood. Merezhkovsky affirms that the Chinese and the Japanese, being the most complete and the most persevering representatives of this " terrestrial " religion, will without fail conquer Europe, where positivism still bears some traces of Christian romanticism. " The Chinese," he says, " are perfect positivists, while the Europeans are not yet perfect Chinese, and, in this respect, the Americans are perfect Europeans." Where is one to look for safety against this heavy load on the understanding and this future humiliation? In socialism, one says. But socialism, if it is not yet bourgeois, is almost so. " The starved proletariat and the rejected bourgeois have different economic opinions," says Merezhkovsky, " but their ideal is the same, the pursuit of happiness." As it is but a step from the prudence of the bourgeois to the exasperated state of the starved proletariat, this pursuit can lead to nothing else but international atrocities of militarism and chauvinism. Progress having become the sole ambition of the cultivated barbarians, satiety became their religion, and the only hope of escaping from this barbarism was to adopt the religion of love, founded by Jesus. Jesus said to those who were treated with violence, and who, in turn, had used violence in trying to free themselves: " Truth (love) will set you free." These words, which identify truth with love, contain in themselves the profoundest social and personal morality. They inspired the first martyrs of Christianity; but in time they were forgotten by the Church. Succumbing to the " diabolical seduction of power," religion itself became a power, an autocracy; people submitted to this power, and thus the Byzantine and Russian orthodoxy came into existence. In this manner, the morals of the government, antichristian in essence, became the doctrine of Christianity; and the particular morals of the latter became transformed into a mysterious gospel of life, relegating its aspirations to an existence beyond the tomb. Now there is nothing for Christianity to do but return to its first sources and develop the principles of universal religion found there. One should no longer be concerned with heavenly and personal advantage, but with earthly affairs and social conditions; instead of being conquered by the government one should conquer it, permeate it with one's spirit, and thus realize the prophecy in the Apocalypse of the millennium of the saints on earth, and destroy the forms of the power of the government, the laws, and the empire. Such a renewal of Christianity demands an energetic struggle, self-forgetfulness, and martyrs. But where is one to find the necessary forces? Merezhkovsky does not see them in the States of western Europe, because the " intellectuals " there are antichristians and are congealed in their bourgeois positivism. " Above these Christian states, above these old Gothic stores," says Merezhkovsky, " rises, here and there, a Protestant wooden cross, half rotted; or a Catholic one of iron, all rusted, and no one pays any attention to them." What purity and nobility remains can manifest itself only in certain scattered individuals, in such great hermits as Nietzsche, Ibsen, Flaubert, Goethe in his old age; they are like deep artesian wells which prove that, beneath the arid earth there is still some flowing water. There is nothing of this sort in Russia. Although backward from the point of view of progress and politics, this country produced the " intellectuals " who form something unique in our present civilization: in essence, they are anti-bourgeois. " The positivism which the Russian ' intellectuals ' have adopted by way of imitation is rejected by their feelings, their

conscience, and their will; it is an artificial
monument that is set up in their minds only."

Merezhkovsky, then, has reason for thinking
that the social renovation of Christianity will
be accomplished in Russia. And as this work
is the especial concern of the clergy, Merezhkovsky, who several years ago was present at
a meeting where the Russian priests affirmed
their desire to free themselves from the yoke
of their religious and secular chiefs, proposed
to accomplish this great mission. "It is indispensable," he says, "for the Russian Church
to untie the knots that bind it to the decayed
forms of the autocracy, to unite itself to the
'intellectuals' and to take an active part in the
struggle for the great political and social deliverance of Russia. The Church should not
think of its own liberty at present, but of martyrdom."

We will not criticize these, perhaps illusory,
ideas and previsions of Merezhkovsky. Russian life has become an enigma; who knows to
what moral crisis the social conscience may be
led by the present political crisis? Merezhkovsky's Olympian æsthetics have made him a for-
eigner in Russian literature. Yet as soon as
the tempest burst forth, certain familiar traits
showed themselves, traits common to the best
Russian writers and to the general spirit of
Russian literature. In his absolute, and even

exaggerated, distaste for " bourgeoisisme," and his desire for an ideal, he is a legitimate son of this literature. The nature of his ideas is in harmony with those we have already found in Tolstoy, with his gospel of Christian anarchism, in Dostoyevsky, with his ideas about the " omni-humanity " of the Russian spirit, in Vladimir Solovyev, with his idea of universal theocracy, and, finally, in Chadayev, one of the most re-markable thinkers of the first half of the last century, who, although now almost forgotten, was the real source of all these ideas.

Thus in the conception of socialized Chris-tianity Merezhkovsky seeks the end of the great antithesis between the " God-man " and the " man-God," between Christ and Bacchus, an antithesis which makes the generality of men often conduct themselves after the manner of that German petty kingdom, of which Heine speaks, where the people, while venerating Christ, do not forget to honor Bacchus by abundant libations. Merezhkovsky's idea ought to appear in the form of a synthetic fusion of the joyous religion of Greece and the religion of love, as taught by Jesus.[15]

VIII

ALEXANDER KUPRIN

The work of Kuprin contrasts strongly with the writings of his predecessors and of his contemporaries. It would be useless to try to connect him with Dostoyevsky, Tolstoy, or Gorky. This does not mean that he came under foreign influence. As a matter of fact his work clearly shows the imprint of Slavic genius and receives its richness from qualities which have always appeared in Slavic literature, — sincerity and accuracy of observation, a passionate love for all manifestations of modern life, lyrical fullness, and power of suggestion. But Alexander Kuprin does not depict adepts of the " religion of pity," nor the psychology of the abnormal, the " pathological case," so curious and rare, and so dear to the author of " Crime and Punishment." [16] He does not reincarnate the sad genius of Korolenko. He is equally separated from Tolstoy and Gorky. He is himself. That is to say, he is an exquisite story-teller, profound and touching,

who imposes neither thesis nor moral upon his
reader, but paints life as it appears to him, —
not seen through the medium of a temperament,
— but in all sincerity, without too much ardor
or too much indifference.

This author was born in 1870. After having
attended the Cadet School and the Military
School at Moscow, he entered military service
as an active lieutenant in 1890, but resigned
seven years later in order to devote his time to
literature. Before this, he had published several stories.

In spite of the undeniable talent which is
found in his earlier writings, the public hesitated to praise him. Certain lucky circumstances, however, favored the beginning of his
work. One of his relatives, at the start, offered him a position on a magazine which she
was then editing. This was a wonderful opportunity for him, for usually at his age the
more gifted writers are still groping around
for light. But merit alone seldom suffices to
form the basis of literary fame. Scandal is
often necessary to consecrate, as one might say,
a growing reputation. Kuprin, without seeking to start a scandal, did so, in spite of himself,
when he published " The Duel," a study of
military life, in which he showed the most absolute impartiality.

To his great surprise, the public accepted

this book as a new indictment of the army. It was because the Manchurian campaign was so recent. Every portrayal of military life passed as a violent satire on the corrupt and disgraced army. Kuprin in vain tried to change this unexpected judgment. As he was an ardent partisan of the theory of " art for art's sake," he could not allow a purpose to be attributed to his work. He had only faithfully portrayed what he had witnessed in the course of his brief career. But in order to strengthen his defence, he alleged reasons which could not be understood in an altruistic country. Besides, several of his stories, such as, " The Wedding," full of the dissolute life led by the officers in their garrisons, " The Inquest," where the author shows the violences to which the Russian soldiers are subjected, " The Night's Lodging," and " The Ensign of the Army," which stigmatize certain lace-bedecked " Lovelaces," only help to nullify his best arguments. In short, his fame spread rapidly and the young writer had to accept the renown that became his.

From that time on Kuprin's road was mapped out. According to the dictates of his fancy he depicts thousands of the ever-changing, different aspects of life. He is equally impelled to write about petty tradesmen, actors, acrobats, and sinners in the Crimea. To the accomplishment of his task, he brings an over-minute and cruel observation. With the genius that is his he dwells on certain important, carefully selected traits of people who live intensely.

In "The Disciple," we see a young sharper on a boat on the Volga. He has the tired eyes of a precocious old man, stubby fingers, and the hands of a murderer alert to strike the fatal blow. He has just fleeced a party of travelers, and he discovers, in a savory conversation with an old cheat, who has found him out, that his soul is being consumed with insatiable desires. And as the old sharper admires the "savoir-faire" of his young friend, the latter observes, not without scorn, that they belong to two very different categories of sharpers. "Among you old fellows," he sneers, "there was romanticism. You loved beautiful women, champagne, music and the song of the tziganes. . . . We, however, we others are tired of everything. Fear and debauch are equally unknown to us. . . ."

After the sharper we have the spy in "Captain Rybnikov." He passes for a Siberian, and says that he has been wounded in the Russo-Japanese war. He goes out into society a great deal, and is most commonly seen in the military offices and in the best "salons" of St.

Petersburg. One night, when he is asleep at a courtesan's house, he mutters the war-cry of Japan: "Banzai! Banzai!" The courtesan denounces him to a policeman who happens to be there, and the pseudo-captain, who is no other than a colonel in the Japanese army, is arrested.

Before leaving the military world, let us analyze "The Delirium." Captain Markov has been ordered by the government to suppress the revolution in certain provinces. Disgusted with the duty of daily executioner, the officer frets himself into a high fever. A non-commissioned officer enters to ask him to decide the fate of three men who have been arrested the previous night, one of whom is an old man with a peaceful and strangely beautiful face. The sergeant knows that they ought to be shot, but these executions are so repulsive to him, that he is anxious to have the sentence of death confirmed by his chief, who seems to him to have the sole responsibility.

"I don't want you ever again to ask me such a question," cries Markov, who has guessed the intention of his subordinate. "You know what you ought to do." And he dismisses him. But the soldier remains motionless.

"What else do you want?" asks the captain.

"The men," answers the stubborn soldier, "are anxious to know what to do with the . . . old . . . man. . . ."

" Get out of here! " the officer roars, exasperated. " Do you understand? "

" Very well, captain. But as to-day is December 31, allow me to offer you my best wishes for a happy New Year."

" Thank you, my friend," replies Markov in a voice which has suddenly become soft.

During the night the captain begins to rave. The old man whom he has just condemned to death appears and speaks to him. He says that his name is Cain, and confesses the murder of his brother. Cursed by God, he wanders disconsolately through the centuries, followed by the groaning of his victim.

Just before dawn the sergeant awakens Markov.

" What about those three men? " asks the captain eagerly.

" Shot, captain! "

" And the old man? The old man? . . . what have you done with him? "

" We shot him along with the others, captain."

The next day Captain Markov asks for his discharge, having decided to leave the army for good.

This story, which is one of the most powerful in Russian literature, would have been enough to bring the young writer renown, even if he had never written anything else. But his work, which is already imposing in amount, abounds in pages of great merit, and especially in well-constructed, brief, tragic stories.

Under this class should be mentioned "Humble People," a short story, the scene of which is laid in the extreme north. It is the story of a close friendship between a nurse in a dispensary and a school-teacher.

Snowed in by a terrible winter — a winter of seven months — these two friends find in their daily meetings the only pleasure that can make their enforced solitude easier for them. However, in spite of their mutual friendship, they often find their lot hard to endure. And they continually quarrel, only to become reconciled almost immediately. But now an unexpected event comes to break the monotony of their existence. They are invited to a dance, given by the priest of the neighboring village, and there they fall in love with two charming young girls, who, they are happy to find, are not indifferent to them. Once at home, they bestow lavish praises on their new friends. With the touching devotion of simple and starved hearts they speak about them as if the young girls already were theirs.

"Mine has eyes of velvet," says the one.

"And mine has hair of pure gold," replies the other.

Gradually, however, their recollections grow

weaker, and fade, just as flowers do. Their
sad life would have begun again if the spring
had not come, and with it brought deliverance.
The two friends, full of new sprightliness, get
up a fishing party one day. A foolish accident
makes them both fall into the river, and they
are drowned.

" The End of a Story," which we are about
to analyze, deserves, as does " Humble People,"
a special place in the work of Kuprin. It is a
little masterpiece of graceful emotion.

Kotik, a child of seven, and the son of a
celebrated painter, teases his father to tell
him a story. The father racks his memory.
He has told so many that his fount is almost
dry.

Suddenly an idea comes to him. Is not his
own life a tender, melancholy, and charming
story? It is not a long time, twelve years at
the most, since he was a poor, obscure painter,
neglected by his masters and tormented by the
miseries of his life. Discouraged, he used continually to curse the hour in which he chose to
devote himself to art. One day, a young girl,
believing in his talent, gave him her hand and
comforted him with her tenderness and angelic
goodness. And love had triumphed.

To-day his name is celebrated among the
most famous, and his paintings adorn the gal-

leries of kings and emperors. The plot of the story is ready.

"Listen," says the father to his son. "There was once upon a time a king who, feeling that he was going to die, gathered his many children about him and said to them: 'I will leave my kingdom to that one of you who can enter a marble palace situated in a very dense forest, and there light his torch from the sacred fire which always burns there. The forest is full of wild beasts and venomous serpents. The palace is guarded by three lions: Envy, Poverty, and Doubt.'

"The young people set out on the road. But, while the older ones search outside of the forest for a road that is not beset with dangers, the youngest courageously starts on the regular path. He there is exposed to many dangers and temptations. Already, his strength failing, he feels that he is almost on the point of succumbing, when a fairy appears and stretches forth her hand to him. The young man blesses this providential aid. The fairy brings back his courage and leads him to the palace."

Near them on the terrace, concealed by some plants, there sat a young and beautiful woman who was eagerly listening to the story. She was Kotik's mother, the fairy of the story, and the favorite pupil of the painter. Some of her paintings had already made a sensation.

The story ended, the father led the child to his room and with the help of his nurse undressed him and put him to bed.

" He had started back towards the terrace, when suddenly two arms embraced his neck, while two sweet lips pressed against his.

" The story was finished."

With these words the story really ends.

Kuprin shows the same grace and the same delicate emotion in his recent story, " The Garnet Necklace," a tale which is analogous to the legend of the troubadour Geoffrey Rudel, which has been made into a play by Rostand in his " Princesse Lointaine."

Geltov, a Russian petty official, loves the beautiful Princess Sheïne with a desperate love. After long hesitation he decides to send her a garnet necklace, with a tender and respectful note enclosed. Alas! his gift is returned to him and the husband of the princess angrily threatens the naïve lover. The latter has not the strength to face the situation, and commits suicide. But before dying he writes to the princess : —

" I saw you for the first time eight years ago in a theatre, and since that time I have loved you with boundless passion. It is not my fault, Princess, that God has sent this great happiness to me. . . . My life for the last eight years

has been bound up in one thought, — you. Believe what I say, believe me because I am going
to die. . . . I am neither a sick man nor an
enthusiast. . . . I consider my love for you
as the greatest happiness that God could have
given me. . . . This happiness I have enjoyed
for eight years. May God give you happiness, and may nothing henceforth trouble
you. . . ."

This naïve and touching letter moves the
princess. At the grave of her unhappy lover,
she recalls the words of an old friend of her
father's: " Perhaps he was an abnormal man or
a maniac. . . . Perhaps, — who knows? —
your life was illumined by a love of which
women often dream, a kind of love that one
does not see nowadays."

One can judge by these summaries how little
Kuprin " pads " his stories. Most of them are
reduced to a commonplace anecdote, which the
author is careful not to ornament in the least.
He respects truth to such a degree that he
offers it to his readers in its disconcerting bareness. He would think that he was failing in
his duty as an observer if he disguised it by
any literary mechanism.

His work, stripped of all general ideas and
of all subjective aspects, is of a rather curious
impersonality. Nothing ever betrays his in-

timate thoughts or feelings. And it is in this
respect that he differs so much from most of
the writers of to-day, who give themselves up
completely to their attractive heroes and vitu-
perate their odious people. Kuprin's objective
tendencies are best shown in his story called
" Peaceful Life."

A retired official, Nassedkine, who has been
enriched by the gratuities which he has exacted
from those who have had to do business with
him, has made it his duty to play censor in his
little town. He makes use of a very discreet
and edifying method: to all of the citizens
whose honor is in danger, he sends one or more
anonymous letters telling them of the " extent
of their misfortune."

Nassedkine has just finished writing two
laconic notes, one of which is to a young
woman whom he tells to visit one of her friends
on a certain day, when, he assures her, her husband is always to be found there. At this moment the church bells ring, and Nassedkine, who
is religious, goes to vespers. On entering, he
notices a fashionable lady, all dressed in black,
in a dark corner of the church. Nassedkine,
more than any one else, knows the heart-rending
story of this woman. She had recently, against
her will, married an excessively rich wood merchant who was almost forty years older than
she. One day, when she thought that her hus-

band had gone off on business, he returned unexpectedly and found her in the arms of one
of his employees. He had been warned that
same morning, by an anonymous letter, that
his wife was deceiving him.

" Beside himself with rage, the merchant
threw his employee out of the house, and then
satiated his brutal jealousy on his wife. He
struck her with his big, hobnailed boots; then
he called his coachman and valet, made her un-
dress completely, and had each of them in turn
lash her beautiful body until, covered with
blood, she fainted away.

" And as the priest at the altar was reciting:
' Lord, I offer Thee the tears of a woman who
has sinned,' Nassedkine repeated this phrase
with satisfaction. Then he left the church in
order to post the two letters he had just written."

This characteristic dryness does not come, as
one is liable to think, from ill-disguised insensi-
bility. Kuprin's soul, on the contrary, is of
such exquisitely fine texture that all human
emotions vibrate there. The few times when he
has expressed himself are enough to convince
the reader. He has often pitied women with a
discreet, fraternal compassion. He has also
devoted many pages to the sufferings of ani-
mals, be it the story of circus horses hurt by
the rolling of the ship, or the story of a kitten

mutilated by wolves. Only a few words are needed to make us tender and to bring tears to our eyes. And it is with the eyes of a poet or a child that he has viewed nature.

No one ever studies a Russian author without finally asking himself what the author's influence was on the political manifestations of society. The answer here is not hard to find: Kuprin, observer, artist, and painter of life, has had no influence. If we except one story, " The Toast," in which he shows his deep affection for the oppressed classes, nothing in his work betrays even slightly his opinions on this subject. Always, the thought of Kuprin deserts the social struggle to fly into more vast and serene surroundings than the theatre of wars and revolutions. And he is doubtless ready to exalt above this terrible struggle, the one thing that he judges eternal, the love of woman.

" There have been kingdoms and kings," he says in his beautiful novel, " Sulamite," " and the only trace that is left of them is the wind in the desert. There have been long and pitiless wars, at the end of which the names of the leaders sparkled like stars: time has effaced all memory of them.

" But the love of a poor girl of the vineyards and a great king [17] will never be effaced and will always live in the minds of men, because love is divinely beautiful, because every woman who loves is a queen, because love is stronger than death."

IX

As we have already noted in the first chapter of this book, Russian literature from 1830 to 1905 is distinctly different from European literature: it is, above all, a literature of action and social propagandas which puts the popular cause in the place of prominence.

This cause has been abandoned by several writers during the last few years. From 1905 to 1910, an evolution, accelerated by the most audacious hopes and the most lively beliefs, has transformed the story and the novel, and has brought to the front certain authors who, up to this time, had scarcely been known. It seems as if suddenly the ancient tradition of Russian literature had been broken. Contrary to the rule of their predecessors, whose thoughts were on justice and liberty, and whose works breathe forth a wholesome quality, a large number of the present writers have been gradually attracted by metaphysical questions, which fill their works with a veritable chaos of morbid conceptions and disenchantment. Some express with acuteness man's unconquerable fear of life or death; others treat of the divine or satanic principles in man; still others study, with a sickly passion, the problems of the flesh in all of its manifestations.[18]

Among the latter, Michael Artzybashev is a writer of great breadth, whose erotic tendencies have spoiled some of his best traits. His novel, " Sanine," which recently caused so much talk, pretends to paint the youth of to-day in Russia. If we believed the author, we should conclude that the above-mentioned youth consisted of hysterical people in whom chastity was the least of virtues.

The heroes of his novel are two representatives of the revolutionary youth, Sanine and Yuri Svagorich. Both of them have deserted " the cause," Sanine, through lassitude, and Yuri, who has met nothing but a despairing indifference among those whom he wanted to save from " the oppression of the shadows," through scorn. Yuri, " a man of the past," is an " intellectual " entirely impregnated with generous altruism, haunted by social and political preoccupations. But he is also a " failure " who falls from one deception into another, because he is thoroughly powerless to combat life.

On the other hand, his friend, Vladimir Sanine, " the man of the future," is, without a doubt, capable of living. None is freer than he from all social and political preoccupations, and none is more than he resolved to obey only his lucid egotism, or the suggestions of his instincts.

These two young fellows meet, one summer, in the country. Yuri lives with his father, a retired colonel; Sanine, with his mother. Sanine's sister, Lida, is in love with the officer Zaroudine, who abandons her later when she is with child. Lida wants to commit suicide, but Sanine stops her and proposes that she marry Dr. Novikov, who has been in love with her for a long time. Parallel to the history of Lida, the life story of Karsavina is presented. Yuri falls in love with this young and pretty schoolteacher. But, although she returns Yuri's love, the young girl, in a moment of passion, gives herself to Sanine, whom she does not love. Disgusted with life, feeling himself weak, neurasthenic, and sick, Yuri, only twenty-six years of age, commits suicide. Karsavina, terribly affected by this act of despair, leaves Sanine. And the latter, after Yuri's funeral, disappears from the city. . . .

All the characters in the book, from Sanine to Karsavina, are continually preyed upon by carnal desires. Long passages of funereal scenes alternate with pictures of the transports of love and the descriptions of masculine and feminine bodies. "Your body proclaims the truth, your reason lies." This is the " leitmotiv " of all the theories that the characters in the book preach.

Let us hasten to add to the praise of the Russian public, that the enormous success of " Sanine " was not justified by the extreme licentiousness of the book, but by the eloquence with which the author claims the right of free love for man and woman.

Although its success was less than that of " Sanine," Artzybashev's second novel, " Morning Shadows," is more interesting and is more realistic than his first.

Tired of their sometimes happy, sometimes monotonous existence, two young people from the provinces, Lisa and Dora, go to St. Petersburg to take some courses there and to join the revolutinary movement. They have read Nietzsche, and want to " live dangerously." In order to realize this project, Lisa has not hesitated to break off her engagement with the charming and naïve Lieutenant Savinov. However, their existence in the capital is nothing but a long and bitter deception: Dora's literary ambitions disappointed! the love of Lisa, who has given herself to the student Korenyev, disappointed! In a fit of despair Lisa kills herself, and her friend, who has not had the courage to follow her example, falls victim to a terrorist outrage which the author describes with rare power.

In his recent novel, " Before Expiration," —
which recalls " Sanine " to our minds again, —
Artzybashev has found some ingenious variations on the old theme, " love and death." The
story of the love affairs of the painter Mikhailov, a cynical and brutal Lovelace who abandons his mistresses when they are with child,
is intermingled incessantly with gloomy episodes, such as the agonies of an old man or of
a child. It is a book for " blasé " people, a
book which a reader with moral health will
not read without a certain feeling of uneasiness.

We are also indebted to Artzybashev for a
series of highly colored stories. " Sub-Lieu-
tenant Golobov," " Blood," " The Workingman
Shevshrev," and " The Millions " are some of
the most remarkable.

Like Artzybashev, but with less talent, Anatol
Kamensky has written little stories happily
enough conceived. Thus, " Laida " — the
story of a worldly woman so taken up with
liberty that she exhibits herself nude before
her husband's guests. Another story called
" Four," tells of four women taken from the
most diverse social classes, ranging from a
young school-girl to the wife of a clergyman,
who give themselves to an officer at the end of
a trip of twenty-four hours. Then there is also

the story of a woman who proposes to an unknown man that he should play a game of cards
with her companions, she being the prize. This
story is called " The Game." Finally, there is
the story of a young man whose agreeable profession consists in living among others gratuitously and in seducing women under the eyes of
their husbands.

These stories are sadly spoiled by a crude
philosophy and by " anarchistic " protestations
against present values.

Certain authors wander into far-away countries for their subjects: to Sodom and Lesbos.
The best known is Michael Kouzmine. This
writer, who happily began with stories of the
Orient in the Middle Ages, has now acquired a
rather sad renown for himself with his story
called " The Wings," which appeared at the end
of 1906. The scandalous success which this
book won, encouraged the author to go on in
the same manner. In poor verse, and especially
in the story, " The Castle of Cards," Kouzmine
has exalted the sin of Sodom as being the most
supreme form of æsthetic emotions.

Closely related to these writers, although
surpassing them all in original talent, Feodor
Sologoub is the most intellectual and subtle of
the Russian modernists. His principal work

consists in depicting the small provincial towns. His heroes are little bourgeois petty officials, school-teachers, and country proprietors.

This chanter of birth and death, disgusted by the banality of existence, has given us, under the title, " The Little Demon," a pathetic picture of human baseness and sordidness, which cannot be read without emotion.

The atmosphere of an arbitrary regime engenders almost always " demonomania." The insecurity of life, and the consecutive injustices in the cavils of the police administration, develop in society a reciprocal fear and distrust. From feeling themselves in danger of being denounced and menaced in their liberty, men rapidly become the prey of terror. And the terrible life, sooner or later, awakens demoniacal terror among the weak. But people of this sort are legion in Russia, and Peredonov, the hero of " The Little Demon," represents this class so graphically that to-day Russian historians and authors designate the era from 1880 to 1905 by the name " peredonovchina." The following is a brief outline of the story:

Peredonov is a school-teacher in a provincial town. His fondest dream is to be nominated primary inspector. He lives with his mistress, the old dressmaker, Varvara by name. One of his mistress's clients, a virtuous and philanthropic princess, makes him understand, one day, that she will have him nominated if he marries Varvara. Peredonov does not love his mistress; he simply lives with her from habit and because she bears, without complaining too much, his coarseness, his cavilling, and his bad humor. However, he will marry her if the princess can get him the position he desires. But will the princess keep her word? It is some time since she has let herself be heard from. What is to be done?

"Marry," says his friend Routilov to him, when he is told the condition of things. "I have three sisters," he continues. "Choose the one you like best and marry her immediately. Thus Varvara will know nothing and cannot throw any obstacles in the way."

"Done!" cries Peredonov, who has known the three sisters for a long time. He chooses the youngest, Valerie.

"Go and tell her about it. I will wait for you in the hall and then we'll go to the priest's together."

Alone, Peredonov again muses: "Doubtless, Valerie is pretty and I shall be happy to have her as my wife. But she is young, pretentious; she will demand lots of new clothes, she will want to go out a lot, in fact, so much that I'll not be able to lay anything aside. Moreover, she'll not look after the kitchen, I'll have poor food, and the cook will rob us." Anguish seizes

him. He knocks at the window, calls his friend,
and says:

" I've changed my mind."

" Ah!" exclaimed the other, horrified.

" Yes, I have reflected, and I have decided
that I prefer the second, Lyoudmila."

Lyoudmila consents, for, besides his personal
fortune, Peredonov occupies an enviable position, and the sisters are poor. She hurriedly
gets dressed; in a quarter of an hour she will
be ready to accompany him to the priest's.

However, Peredonov reflects: " Lyoudmila is
pretty and plump; she doubtless has a perfect
body, but she is always jolly, she loves to laugh.
She will laugh incessantly and will make her
husband seem ridiculous." Full of fear, he
knocks at the window: " I have reflected," he
cries. " I prefer the oldest, Darya."

" What an awful man!" cries his friend.
" Hurry up, Darya, or he'll leave all of us in
the lurch."

Again Peredonov reflects: " Darya is nice,
not young any more, and economical; she knows
life. But . . . she is decisive in her resolu-
tions, and she has an energetic character. She
is not the kind who would listen to my observations. She could make life hard for me, and
use me ill. Frankly, do I have to marry any of
the three sisters? What will the princess say
when she hears of my marriage? And my posi-

tion as inspector? How stupid it is to stand waiting in this court! Without a doubt, Routilov ensnared me. I've got to get out of this at any cost!"

He spits on all sides to conjure up the spirits, then knocks at the window, and tells the amazed family:

"I am going away. . . . I have thought it over. I don't want to get married."

Meanwhile, his position in school becomes intolerable; complaints are registered against him; he is reproached with having ill-treated and even with having beaten the poor children, and with treating the noble and rich children with too much respect. His ridiculous and evil passions cause him to be detested by all. Luckily, he will soon be nominated inspector, and then he will say good-bye to all this riffraff. In the meantime, Varvara writes a letter, filled with the most alluring promises, to which she signs the princess's name, and has it mailed from St. Petersburg. Peredonov is at the height of joy; but, being a prudent man, he does not want to marry before he has received the nomination. He waits and waits for it, and, meanwhile, he is not even sure of his position in the school. He discovers enemies everywhere, and believes there are always spies at his heels. In order to cajole the administration, he begins to frequent the church, and to pay visits to the

city authorities. He assures the chief of police
of his respect, and, in order to give a glaring
proof of his devotion to the established institutions, he lodges information against a school-
mistress of the locality. But still the nomination does not come, and he lives in a continual
trance. The evil in him increases. He torments
beasts and human beings. He whips his pupils,
throws nettles at his cat, and maltreats his cook.
He believes himself more and more in the
power of the demon, and terrible visions follow
him:

" He saw running before him, a little, grey,
noisy beast. It sneered, its head trembled, and
it ran quickly around Peredonov. When he
wanted to seize it, it escaped under the cup-
board, only to reappear a moment later. . . ."

This strange book, written with rare perfection, had a great success. To several readers
who thought that they recognized the author
himself in the person of Peredonov (Sologoub
had had the same position as his hero for several
years) the author replied in the preface of a
recent edition, by these malicious lines:

" Men like to be loved. They adore noble
and elevated descriptions and portrayals. They
even search among the scum for a ' divine
spark.' They also are surprised and offended
when any one offers them a veracious and sombre
picture. And most of them then do not fail to

declare: ' The author has described himself in
his work.' But no, my dear friends and
readers, it is you, and only you, whom I have
painted in my book, ' The Little Demon.' "

In " The Charms of Navii " Sologoub happily blends fantasy and reality. Revolutionary
meetings alternate with improbable hypnotic
seances, and terrible cortèges of corpses contrast violently with scenes of platonic and
ethereal love.

The plot of the story, " The Old Home," is
not less distressing than the preceding one. A
young revolutionary, condemned to death by
court-martial, has been executed, but for his
dear ones this death has never been a reality.
His mother and sister, and even the old servant,
have not the strength to admit his disappearance. They wait and wait for his return until
their own death carries them off.

Another story, " The Crowd," shows us a
" fair " at which pewter goblets are being given
away. These so excite the greediness of the
crowd that a fray results, in which three children are seriously wounded. While dying, the
unfortunates have terrible visions of life and
humanity. " It seemed to them that ferocious
demons were chuckling and sneering silently
behind human faces. And this masquerade
lasted so long that the poor little tots thought
that it would never end. . . ."

Sologoub is, above all, a chanter of death.
Almost all of his works unveil a murder, suicide,
or madness. Moreover, the author, who shows
only the injustices, evils, and infamy of life,
and who affirms that the only happiness that he
foresees for man is the possibility of " creating
for himself a chimera " by turning away from
reality, finds the clearest colors and the sweet-
est expressions in speaking of death.

" There is not a surer and more tender friend
on earth than death," says one of his heroes.
" And if men fear the name of death, it is because they do not know that it is the real life,
eternal and invariable. Life deceives very often,
death never. It is sweet to think of death, as
it is to think of a dear friend, distant and yet
always close at hand. . . . One forgets all in
the arms of the consoling angel, the angel of
death."

The ever supremely correct and beautiful
language of Sologoub shows the power of a
master, and it is most regrettable that an artist
of his merit should confine himself to so morbid
an art.

These then are the principal authors — some
of whom have enjoyed an immense popularity
— who treat the " cursed questions : " the rights
of the flesh, the problem of death, and other
equally " cursed " problems.

The other writers are principally occupied
with social questions, and, without rigorously
following in the steps of their predecessors, remain, however, most of the time, realists.

Among these, Sergyev-Tzensky occupies a
prominent place. The stories of this writer
show us beings who seem strangers to what is
going on around them. This peculiarity comes
from the fact that Tzensky does not understand
the physical facts in the same way that the natu-
ralists do. For him, they are the manifestations
of the will of a supernatural entity, incomprehensible, inconceivable, and, at the same time,
clearly hostile to man.

His story, " The Sadness of the Fields," tes-
tifies to this singular conception. A farmer and
his wife, good and peaceful people, have for
many years wished for a child. Up to this
time, the six children which the mother has
given birth to have died in their infancy. They
are anxiously awaiting the seventh. Will this
one live? Will not the sadness of the fields,
which puts its imprint on everything, kill it as
it has killed the others? Alas! the child is not
viable, and the mother dies in child-birth. They
are buried, and " the fields and the surrounding
country forever keep their powerful and mysterious melancholy."

" The Fluctuation " is one of the most curious and beautiful of all of Tzensky's stories.

Anton Antonovich, a rich and enterprising merchant, of a very violent and unruly character,
lives like a wolf in his domains, alone with his
family, without seeing any of his neighbors.
The peasants detest him. As his partners and
helpers, he always engages nonentities, without
power of initiative, who blindly follow his
orders. Intellectual and energetic men cannot
get along with him. Men, beasts, and nature
in its entirety, are considered by this man as
having been especially created for his service.
The one end of his life is wealth and power.
The only beings he loves are his wife and his
three sons; but even they have to bow down
to his will.

One day, he buys some straw and insures it
against fire. Sometime later, it burns. They
accuse him of having been the incendiary.
Ridiculous accusation! He is a millionaire and
the straw barely cost a few hundred rubles.
The old man makes fun of the whole affair; he
insults the judge, his own lawyer, and even the
jury. He feels the impending misfortune, but
his inborn violence carries him away from prudence. He is condemned to hard labor and he
succumbs to a sickness that he has been feeling
coming on for a long time. He had made a
pillager's nest for himself, and he died like a
pillager, abandoned even by those who were
dear to him.

In Tzensky's short stories, " I Shall Soon
Die," " Diphtheria," " Tedium," and " The
Masks," there is something mysterious, fatal,
and terrible that constantly surrounds his
people. As to his longer works, " The Swamp
in the Forest," and " Lieutenant Babayev,"
they plunge the reader into the mad chaos of
the often abnormal emotions felt by the characters. These characters imagine the divine
side of human nature; they consider it as
having existed before in the essence of things,
but the reality does not harmonize with their
dream. The authentication of this discord
torments Tzensky's heroes and their souls pro-
test passionately, but in vain, against these
outrages.

Sergyev-Tzensky's style, graphic and pure,
often strange, has found imitators among the
younger writers. Thus, Mouyzhel, who describes village life, is visibly influenced by his
writings. Acording to him, the soul goes
through life without understanding it, without
being able to ascribe any meaning to it. And
he is so sincere, that his works obtain the frank-
est sort of success.

While Mouyzhel studies peasant life, Simon
Youshkevich, to the exclusion of all else, makes
a study of the poor Russian Jews. Some of
his stories have produced an overwhelming im-

pression. They show us beings, heaped up, pell-mell in the ghettos of the cities of western and southern Russia, dirty and unwholesome ghettos, where consumption and all kinds of terrible sickness reign. These stories, often tragic, always sad, have given Youshkevich the name of " chanter of human suffering."

In his earlier works — the best of which are " The Jews," " Tavern-Keeper Heimann," " The Innocents," " The Prologue " and " The Assassin " — he devoted himself to portraying, not isolated persons, but the immense Russian Jewish proletariat, with its sad past, its bloody present, and its exalted faith in the future. Youshkevich has created this sphere; he considers the poor people of the cities not as a social class, but as a symbolic representation of an entire organization. If his work is at times infected with romanticism and some exaggeration the reader will gladly forget these imperfections when he recognizes the fact that they are necessary to enable this author to express the truth. What makes this writer unique, is that he cannot be confounded with any one else. He has never influenced any of his readers and, in turn, has never imitated any one. He made himself what he is.

His last literary productions — with the exception of his very touching drama, " Misere " — have been inferior to his former work. But

the abundance of the materials furnished by
Jewish life would still give this author opportunity to give us more of the magnificently
colored pictures that he gave us in his initial
productions.

Close to Youshkevich should be placed the
two young writers, Sholom Ash and Izemann.
Sholom Ash has principally depicted the Jewish
world and its psychology. " The God of Ven-
geance " is a touching picture of the life of
young Jewish girls who have been obliged to
prostitute themselves for a living. " Sabbatai-
Zevi," [19] a philosophical poem, treats of the
powerful personality of that Jewish prophet and
of the surroundings in which he passed his
life.

Izemann, who has written quite a few tales
and stories, is a very uneven author. His best
work is " The Thorn Bush," a drama of the
life of the Russian-Jewish revolutionists.
Manousse, the son of a poor tinsmith, has
been arrested, and then hanged for having taken
part in a terrorist uprising. His sister, Dara,
engaged to the son of a wealthy manufacturer,
has, in her turn, been killed at a barricade. She
is carried back to her home, and there, revolver
in hand, the mother receives the soldiers. She
falls mortally wounded at the side of her
fourteen year old son. Thus, the entire
family perishes. The last act of this sombre

drama makes a tremendous impression on the stage.

After having been a country doctor for several years, Eugene Chirikov abandoned his practice in order to devote himself to literature. His drama, " The Jews," has aroused great interest and has been played with great success both in Russia and abroad. It is one of the most significant works of this writer. The story concerns itself with the children of a poor Jewish watchmaker, who are infatuated with ideas of progress. Their infatuation is such, that the daughter becomes engaged to a Gentile. A delirious mob invades the houses of the Jews. The store of the poor watchmaker is not spared, and the fiancée of the Gentile is ravished and then murdered. The rapid action of the play makes it a dramatic " slice of life."

The other plays and stories of this author give us pictures both of the petty " bourgeois " and of the " intellectuals." Thus, " The Strangers " tells the story of a group of " intellectuals " who have strayed into a small market town in the provinces where all are hostile to them. Then there is " The Invalids," which gives the story of the life of an old man who, after having been exiled to Siberia for several years on account of " advanced " ideas, returns to Russia as confident as ever, ready to conse-

crate the rest of his life to the people. Finally,
" At the Bottom of the Court," " The Mysteries
of the Forest " and " Marya Ivanovna " are
dramas from bourgeois life, while " The
Sorceress " is a play, taken from a national
epic.

Not less well known than Chirikov, is Ossip
Dymov. He forsook the " Imperial Institute
of Foresters " in order to devote himself to
literature. He has written numerous stories,
among which " Vlass " is the most captivating.
It is the childhood of Vlass told by himself. An
observing little person, the child notices everything and everybody around him. His father
had killed himself before the child was old
enough to talk, and his mother, a very intelligent and stern woman, alone had to care for
four children. Vlass has an older brother, Yuri,
a sister, Olya, and a younger brother, Vladimir,
a kind and inoffensive creature. Life runs
along smoothly in the little country town. The
days pass, one like the other, and the most insignificant event takes on grave importance in
this monotonous life. One night, Vlass's young
teacher is arrested and sent to Siberia. A year
later, a friend of the family, who has been in
exile a long time, comes back secretly and passes
several days at the house. Later on, it is " the
beautiful, good aunt " who comes unexpectedly ;
but she soon departs, leaving a mass of confused

and restless thoughts in the child's mind. Vlass
ends his story with a most pathetic account.
Far away from the little town, in one of the
prisons of St. Petersburg, they are going to
hang Yuri. The entire family has broken down
since they have heard the news, and they sit up
the night before the execution, trying, in
thought, to alleviate the torment of their cher-
ished one.

In his other stories, the author paints nature
in an original and entirely personal manner.
According to a Russian critic, the works of
Dymov breathe forth " the fresh breeze and the
quickening aroma of the forests."

Dymov has also written some very well-liked
plays, of which " Niyu " is the most original.
Niyu, a young woman, abandons her husband
and child in order to follow a poet, whose beautiful language and touching poetry have won
her admiration and brought her under his spell.
She hopes that her lover will create a new world,
a higher and nobler world than the every-day
one, because he is a poet, that is to say, one of
the elect. The abandoned husband and the un-
cared-for child desperately call out for their
wife and mother. In vain! However, the days
that she passes with the poet are filled with disenchantment, disillusion, and bitterness. Despairing, she writes a letter to her old parents
who live in a distant town, and then commits

suicide. And hardly is Niyu buried, when the
poet, although sadly affected by the premature
loss of his companion, again begins to charm
and entrance by his beautiful words other
women, whose lives he ruins.

" Niyu " has had a tremendous success, because it brings a really new formula into
the theatrical world. Very little action, very
few " situations ; " no artificial procedure: life;
dialogue imitated from reality; an atmosphere of despair and tedium in which three
beings cruelly struggle; sincere evolution, very
much pessimism, and happiness and love, constitute the traits that characterize this very
human piece of writing.

Mention should also be made of Sayitzev, certain of whose stories are comparable to the
aquarelles of a landscape painter. One of his
best works is " Agrafena," a touching picture
of the life of a peasant woman. During her
lifetime, she was a domestic in the cities, and
when finally, bent under years of labor, she
comes back to her native village and her
daughter, whom she has secretly brought up at
great pains, it is only to find that she has committed suicide, having been abandoned by her
lover.

Among others, should be mentioned Gussev-
Orenburgsky, who has written some very inter-

esting stories about the Russian clergy; Skita-
letz, whose " Rural Tribunal " has had a great
success, and has been translated into several
languages; Seraphimovich and Teleshov, who,
like Chirikov, depict the life of the " intellectuals," and Olizhey, the psychologist of revolutionary spheres, known particularly by his
" The Day of Judgment," which tells of an
officer, a member of a council of war, who is
forced to condemn his future brother-in-law to
death. This story leaves an indescribable impression of terror and horror.

Let us finally mention Count Alexis Tolstoy,
the homonym of the great Russian thinker, to
whom the critics predict a brilliant future. His
first work appeared in 1909. He generally depicts landed proprietors. His recent stories,
" The Asking in Marriage," and " Beyond the
Volga," show signs of great strength and power
of observation.

Among the women, there are three who show
real talent. In fact, Mme. Hippius-Merezhkov-
skaya is regarded as one of the founders of
Russian modernism. We are indebted to her
for some rather daring verses and some very
good stories. The most recent of these, " The
Creature," is the curious history of a love-sick
prostitute; " The Devil's Doll " is an episode in
the life of the Russian " intellectuals." En-

dowed with a caustic spirit, she excels all others
in literary criticism.

Then comes Mme. Verbitzkaya, who has declared herself a champion of women, who, she
thinks, should throw off the often tyrannical
yoke of their husbands. Her novels, " Va-
vochka," and " The Story of a Life," have
given her just renown. In " The Spirit of the
Time " she has tried, not without some success,
to paint the immense picture of the revolution of 1905. Her recent novel, " The Keys
of Happiness," has had an enormous success.

Finally, mention should be made of Mme.
Shepkina-Koupernik, who has written some
verses and charming stories, full of caressing
tenderness and delicate psychology. Her
stories, in which she shows us two old Italian
masters, are very interesting. Thus, " Eternity
in a Moment " is delicious. In a painter's
studio, a young model by chance meets her old
lover, who has also been reduced to posing in
studios. Happy at heart, the woman rushes
toward him, but he pushes her away: he is too
miserable, he has fallen too low to dare to love
her again. Repulsed by him, she stands as if
petrified, with death in her soul, and her face
changed by terrible despair. At this moment
the master enters; he looks at the young
woman and utters a cry of joy; finally he has

found what he wants for his picture: human traits ravaged by suffering and despair!

Russia is also indebted to this author for impeccable translations of Rostand's "Princesse Lointaine" and "Chantecler."

THE END

NOTES

[1] Tolstoy.

[2] This spelling has been adopted here, rather than Chekhov, since it is more familiar to the public. In all other cases, the *ch* and *v* have been retained.

[3] In many European papers there is always to be found a part called the "feuilleton," which usually consists of a serial story, continued from day to day.

[4] For some reason, unknown to the translator, the author has made no mention of Tchekoff's famous play, "The Sea-Gull." This drama, which, when first produced, was a flat failure, scored a tremendous success a short while afterwards. It is especially interesting in that the author has made one of the characters, Trigorin, largely autobiographical. To-day "The Sea-Gull" is one of the most popular productions on the Russian stage.

[5] On the continent of Europe, a university degree between that of bachelor and of doctor.

[6] In Russian, Gorky means bitterness.

[7] This was preceded by a story called " The Devil."

[8] A celebrated brigand in the time of Ivan the Terrible who, in order to be pardoned, conquered Siberia in the name of the Tsar.

[9] This passage is a sort of a variation on the theme that Poe has developed in a masterful way in his poem, " The Bells."

[10] In the English translation this book is called " A Dilemma."

[11] Mention should be made of some of Andreyev's other dramas: " To the Stars," " Anfissa," " Gaudeamus," and " Sava," plays of uneven value, but with a strength of observation and analysis which is not inferior to that shown in some of his best stories.

[12] Also called " The Romance of Leonardo da Vinci, the Forerunner."

[13] Russian noblemen.

[14] In Russia, the name of the biblical Ham has become synonymous with servility and moral baseness. Merezhkovsky employs this scornful term to designate those people who are strangers to the higher tendencies of the mind and are entirely taken up with material interests. His " Ham Triumphant " is the Antichrist, whose reign, as predicted by the Apocalypse, will begin with the final victory of the bourgeoisie. In one chapter of this book, Merezhkovsky proves that the writers of west-

ern Europe and Russia (Byron and Lermontov) err in crowning this Antichrist with an aureole of proud revolutionary majesty, for, since he is the enemy of all that is divine in man, he can only be a character of shabby mediocrity and human banality, that is to say, a veritable "Ham."

[15] Merezhkovsky has also written a long historical drama, called "The Death of Paul I." He traces there, with his accustomed animation, the figure of the weak and criminal Tsar, now heaping favors upon those who surround him, now persecuting them with the most terrible cruelty. The savage scene of the assassination of this tyrant is of remarkable beauty.

[16] Dostoyevsky.

[17] Refers to Solomon.

[18] Happily, this literary crisis seems to have been ephemeral. Since the beginning of 1910, according to a Russian critic, "the salubrity of the atmosphere" has been accomplished. The "cursed questions" are less prominent in recent works, and it seems that the crisis which desolated Russian literature for several years has come to an end, and that the writers are going back to the old traditions of Russian literature.

[19] A famous impostor of the 17th century: 1626-1676.